MOO·LAH·GY

MOO·LAH·GY

uncovering the secret cash cow hidden in your brand

Kelly Lucente

BUBBLE
PRINT
PRESS

Jacket Design by Re-Tool Marketing
Illustrations by Amanda Cox of Re-Tool Marketing
Photography by Annie Marie of Annie Marie Photography

Production/Editing by Bubble Print Press

ISBN-13: 978-0-692-59362-2
LCCN: 2016900855

Bubble Print Press
Minneapolis, MN
www.bubbleprintpress.com

for joey

FOREWORD

By: Ken Kragen

Nationally Acclaimed Hollywood Entertainment Manager
Creator of *We Are the World* and *Hands Across America*

Congratulations! You've just made an excellent decision. You're looking at this book and considering whether to buy it–or you've already done so. Either way you're on the cusp of a wonderful and invaluable experience. If you haven't already, I hope you'll take the next step and get it. It's a terrific read and full of great concepts that illustrate the importance of brand and techniques of branding that will help you set your business apart from all the other businesses out there just like yours. Kelly Lucente threads throughout this book all sorts of personal stories from her wonderful career, the good, the bad, and the ugly to let you know you are not alone and to give you insight on the pitfalls to avoid as you carve your own business path.

In her introduction, Kelly says *"you'll find much of this book entertaining."* I learned one thing years ago, teaching a marketing course at UCLA: the best way to get anyone to learn anything is to entertain them. In fact, there's a true story about a teaching experiment that used a classic physics instructor with total knowledge of the subject to teach one class and an entertaining comedic actor to teach the exact same material to a similar class. Those in the entertaining class learned far more than those in the standard professor's class.

Here you get the best of both. This is a book that is totally entertaining while being completely informative. That's because Kelly herself is first and foremost fun and enthusiastic, while at the same time being one of the most knowledgeable and creative brand marketers in the world.

I know firsthand about entertainment, having spent the majority of my long career managing some of the biggest names in the business, including Kenny Rogers, Lionel Richie, Olivia Newton-John, the Bee Gees, Burt Reynolds, Trisha Yearwood, The Smothers Brothers, and many others.

I've also put together several of the largest and most historic humanitarian events of all time, including We Are The World, Hands Across America, NetAid, and parts of Live Aid and President Clinton's first inauguration.

Along the way in my charmed career I've picked up an MBA from Harvard Business School; received the United Nations Peace Medal; and garnered several MTV Awards and lots of experience branding and marketing individuals, companies, and projects, so I know a bit about the subject of brand and the value it can have on a business.

I've also mentored Kelly and must say she is one of the best students I've ever had. The minute I met her, I knew she was something special, and not only have we become great friends, I've enjoyed watching her give back and help others with her gifts and limitless energy—which is highly contagious, I might add. Just being around her stirs creative juices and I've seen people be the better for it.

I couldn't possibly recommend Kelly and her ideas any more strongly. She knows her stuff and she's committed to sharing it with others in the hopes that entrepreneurs and small business owners can glean insights that will help them propel their businesses to a different level as a result of understanding this mysterious thing called "brand." Read this book, enjoy it, and apply the terrific principles. You won't regret it!

Ken Kragen

PREFACE

When I was fifteen years old, I received my first dose of cold, hard reality about the power of brand and I did not even know I was being schooled at the time. While other kids were doing their homework and practicing the clarinet, I was drawing. As luck would have it, I was commissioned to create a poster for the local Lion's Club chapter's Corn Festival. What a thrill, I was a working artist! Keep in mind that this was thirty-three years ago and there were no computers, no cellphones, or Photoshop. All "creative" was done by hand . . . especially if you were a young girl in rural Minnesota with a shared telephone line, and not a graphic designer in a swanky agency in downtown Minneapolis commiserating over national brand ad campaigns like on *Mad Men*.

I had done the Lion's Club poster the year before to rave reviews, so I felt like a pro going into my second year of "designing" for them. Only, this time, it was a wee bit different. The previous year I had some-one assist me with the typography, formatting the words on the poster. However, this year I was on my own. My competence was in my drawing ability, not in stylizing copy, but I did not realize it would be a problem until after I had created the poster. You see, back then you had one shot. One draft. One "take" to get it right. The Lion's Club provided the poster paper, so there were no do-overs or edits possible.

Once I had completed the poster that particular year someone told me something I will never forget, *"When you are writing letters, be consistent. Either use all uppercase or all lowercase. Never mix the two within the same word."* I had NO idea! Why hadn't I been told that before? Nowhere had I read that in a book, but after seeing the truth on the page in per-manent marker the mistakes were glaring. It was as if they were screaming at me. But there was no going back. I was on a deadline and I had to submit the piece as it was. I was embarrassed. Needless to say, I was beyond disappointed—but not surprised—when I attended the Corn Festival and saw someone else's work on the flyers. I was never asked to submit again.

My lesson was a painful one that day. Beyond the bruised ego, I realized the details meant everything. It didn't matter how good my overall design was or that the signature scarecrow I had created for them the year before had been turned into swag. It was the sum of the parts that gave the overall impression—and poor typography was the kiss of death on the project. Even though the Osmond's might say, *"One bad apple don't spoil the whole bunch."* The sad truth is in this case it did. As a young girl, I had no idea—and that's the point: we don't know what we don't know. I wish I would have gotten that typography advice prior to my putting pen to paper, but that didn't happen.

There have been many lessons for me along the way, but that one sticks with me as a reminder to look closer, to check and double check, and to realize that anything less than *"we've considered and addressed it all"* doesn't leave the shop. Now that I own a branding agency and have had a couple of decade's worth of experience, I can "see" and, seeing—really seeing and understanding—is key.

And so goes brand today . . . and the importance of it. It needs to be looked at holistically and not simply glanced at to verify its aesthetics. How does it make you feel? What experience does it evoke through its look, tone, and feel? Any one thing that's off could mean the difference between a "no" and a "yes" and in sales, that's really big deal. *Right?* After all, without sales, what do you have?

INTRODUCTION

From as early as I can remember, I've been a brand snob—but not a snob in the way you might think. Not the "I'm cool because I have it" kind of way, but in the "Oh my gosh, how cool is that?" sort of way. I found myself mesmerized by all the popular toys. I didn't like Barbie because of her figure. I liked her because she was "Barbie" and she had "friends." Who had Barbie's dream house? Who had her car? Did Ken drive? If you had a Barbie, you could play out what it would be like to be a teenager right on the floor of your second-grade, seven-year-old bedroom. You could dress her in all the latest fashions, have her babysit and walk the dog, attend a gala, and take a trip on an airplane all in one day!

Knockoff dolls didn't quite pack the same punch. They weren't Barbie. They were a yawner.

Crayola is still my favorite brand of crayon. Why? Because nothing colors like a Crayola. Don't believe me? I dare you to do a test. Buy a generic brand, then have some children color with both of them. Then, ask for their feedback. The beautiful thing about having children be your focus group is they are typically brutally honest so consider this food for thought for any future beta testing ideas you might have. Children might give you the answers you seek. (Or, you could just take my word for it.) Not only is Crayola's "crayon" quality the best I believe you'll find, but they live their brand by continually finding ways of being creative. In 1993, for their ninetieth anniversary, they allowed consumers to name their colors through a "Name the New Colors" contest.[1] One of the winners was called "Macaroni and Cheese" and, believe it or not, it's still in production today. Genius? Absolutely. I actually submitted a name to that contest. I can't remember what I submitted, but I didn't win. I think there's a definite correlation between those two factors:

Crayon Name + Not Memorable = Doesn't Win.

I'll never forget Tonka trucks. Tonka trucks were good quality. My brother was a bruiser (and he cut

 my hair, but I digress). When he was little, he was as wide as he was tall. Actually, he was kind of built like a Tonka truck, really, and he played rough, so his toys needed to be able take a beating. Tonka could stand up to the test and, since we lived in the same house, I had plenty of exposure to the product myself. I watched as he played for hours with those trucks, power driving them into walls and launching them off balconies. (I think Barbie may have taken a spin or two around the living room . . . and off the balcony.) Because we lived in Minnesota, near the Tonka toy production facility, when I was a bit older I had the opportunity to tour the plant. It was fascinating to see the products roll down an assembly line with workers acting very much like Santa's elves. Seeing the back end of their brand shed new light on my appreciation for the front end.

The lesson for me in my later years was proof of concept (that the product, in fact, worked) created raving fans—and repeat buyers. In fact, since its inception, Tonka has sold more than 250 million trucks.[2] I imagine even Santa would be pleased.

For me, brand has always gone beyond the actual product. This might sound strange, but television commercials have always been way more appeal ing to me than the actual programs. When I was young and the show was on, I was busy being busy but when the commercials came on and everyone else took potty breaks and refilled the chip bowl, I was transfixed. It was almost as if I was teleported into the TV itself, living out the commercial with the actors, drinking in the promise of whatever they were selling. Oh, the joy! It was like Christmas every fifteen minutes. The same scenario happens for me today, as an adult, much to the dismay of my family who always want to be a bit too chatty when I want to concentrate. Commercials tell me secrets I share with my clients. Why do I share them? Because my clients and I can learn many lessons from the big guys. They pave the way, so we can walk the worn path—if we listen and we learn.

IS THIS BOOK FOR **YOU?**

Sometimes I wonder if I'm reading the right book, if the author was thinking about me when it was written. So I know what you're thinking because I've thought it, too: "So What?" Well, this book is filled with answers to that question and, as you read, you'll also say, "I had no idea!" This book is filled with answers to your "So What?" because I've spent my career figuring it out and answering it for myself. I'm here to pass my experiences on to you, so you can avoid the potholes I've face-planted into throughout my career.

If you are a business owner who wants to understand how to make money without having to turn yourself inside out explaining and re-explaining, cajoling and convincing, distracting and romancing so your audience sees you, then this book is for you. It will show you how to build a brand that gets noticed—without having to stand on your head.

WHY **NOW?** WHY **THIS BOOK?**

The answers are simple. You can make money by understanding the power of brand and implementing that knowledge. How? By connecting the dots for your audience. If dots don't connect, or if they don't make sense, consumers pause—and a pause is a "no." I'll show you how to eliminate the "no" and make it really easy for your audience to say "yes." By getting inside the heads of your ideal customers and speaking their language, you'll get more than a "yes." They'll write you a check. If it's clear and they get you, if you are honest and they know you care, they will trust you.

Brand = trust.
Trust = money.

> **❝**
>
> # TRUST
>
> a firm belief in the **reliability, truth, ability** or **strength** of someone or something.

I wish there had been a one-stop resource for me when I was fifteen and working on my Lion's Club-commissioned poster. I wish I would have known it's easier to say "yes" when it's clear, instead of the way I was taught in sales—you simply needed to churn through several "no" responses before you'll get a "yes."

So, if you are a business owner wanting to build a "gotta-have-it" brand, let's do something about it. Turn the page, sharpen your pencil, and eat your Wheaties. We've got some rowing to do!

SIDE NOTE:

When I crack the binding on a business management book for the first time, I often wonder if there is an ideal way to consume the information. I thumb through the table of contents (if there is one) and try to find insight on shortcuts because I find I simply want the answers—as quickly as possible.

With that in mind, I've written this book in my voice, from my perspective, and based upon my learnings over the past thirty-plus years. We will be going through a lot of information, but we'll be getting you to the answers as quickly as you can go. (I wasn't kidding about the Wheaties.) I've tried to keep it visual, and to help break up the headiness of the content—and hopefully you'll find much of it entertaining. Watch for the "So What?" in each chapter. This is the big "a-ha" for that section and will often be the "answer" and main takeaway as you go.

Throughout the book, I mention resources, so use them if you can. I rarely make those kinds of suggestions unless I feel they've hit a homerun. So, if I mentioned something, I think it's a keeper.

If you can, read the book from start to finish (in that order) because the process is chronological. And really use this book. Dog-ear the corners, tab if you can, highlight the text, and write in the margins. My hope for you is this book will become the one on the shelf with the most wear because you refer to it often.

Okay, so that's it. Let's do this!

CHAPTER **ONE**

FISH WHERE THERE ARE FISH.

When I first dipped my toe into a thing called sales, it was for a national homebuilder. I had no formal training other than the three weeks I had spent getting my real estate license. During those three weeks, I watched instructor after instructor jump from desk to desk to find creative ways to keep our attention and our eyes on the prize: getting licensed by passing on the first try so we could get in the field and start selling homes. Ironically, the material we were tested on was a bit obsolete and our instructors shared that with us numerous times, telling us over and over to just memorize to pass—then forget what we learned. The good news for me was that I wasn't selling existing real estate, but working for a builder (and builders are completely different). The bad news was I didn't have any builder training. I was plopped into a neighborhood with twenty-four completed homes and told to sell them. I wasn't given a sales manual or any training on new home sales. It was all Greek to me and I found myself stumbling through the process using trial and error.

I learned pretty quickly that in order to sell an attached townhome with a micro-sized single car garage only big enough to hold a Ford Focus, a home that came with only basic features and was built on a cabbage patch, I needed to get really good at selling a thing I like to call "differentiation" (I cover this term in-depth in chapter 2). I had to become an expert at addressing the uniqueness of each home even though it was jam-packed in a sea of the same. I needed to figure out—and fast—a way to be an authority on not only the efficiency of a small garage, but also the value of cabbage in the soil.

A brand is no longer what **we** tell the consumer it is - it is what the consumers tell **each other** it is.

SCOTT COOK | FOUNDER OF INTUIT

I even took to trying to figure out how to sell a step further when I found myself at a new site that bordered two freeways and had been built under industrial-sized power lines. (You've seen them, right? The towers that are the size of skyscrapers that snap, pop and buzz all day long?) I needed to figure out how to sell the homes directly beneath those lines. So I called the city and got all of the research I could on those monster power lines. I had a file drawer full of data that supported the fact that those power lines didn't give off any more radiation than an alarm clock sitting on your nightstand right next to your head. I was ready for battle. When my first young family walked into my sales trailer, I was armed and more than prepared. When they opened with "So tell us about those power lines," I immediately pulled out the file, showed them all the data, explained that the power lines were, in fact, safe to live under, and suggested they make sure they moved their alarm clock to a different location in their bedroom. I felt so empowered. I knew more about those lines than any of my co-workers. And then this happened: the young couple with their two toddler children in tow looked at me in horror and said, "We just thought they were ugly."

That moment was a major epiphany for me regarding brand. You see, it didn't matter what I thought about those power lines. What mattered was what the customer thought about them and I hadn't given them a chance to tell me what they thought. I immediately tried to impress upon them my views. My opinion. My ideas. You see, in branding, customers decide—not us as business owners. We need to take a minute, get in the heads of our audience, and really understand what they want and need—and then deliver on that request. It doesn't matter whether or not we think our widget will change their lives. It matters what they think. Needless to say, I didn't sell that young couple a home that day and the file drawer remained closed the rest of my time at that location.

Remember, brand is a *they* game.

SO, WHAT IS **BRAND** ANYWAY?

I have found that as hot as the word "brand" is in the marketplace—and even with the constant buzz around it—very few people really understand what in the world it means and why they should care. As much as I hear about the importance of brand through an abundance of daily social content, I would think everyone on the planet would have an absolute understanding, but they don't. Do you want to know why they don't? Because even though brand is easy to articulate, it's very difficult to completely understand because brand is a feeling, not a tangible result like the answer to a math problem—not to mention feelings change (sometimes like the wind). Feelings aren't static and they aren't absolute. So when people are considering brand, they can change their minds—and they often do. For someone trying to control and manage a brand, it's an endless black abyss of uncertainty . . . until it's certain. Then it shifts, and we, as branders, have to shift again.

This hard-to-encapsulate thing called "brand" is ever changing and evolving. It's difficult to catch and as soon as you do, brand slips from your fingers and you're back in the race. It's kind of like herding cats. It can be frustrating, exhausting, and—for people like me—exhilarating. But, I do this for a living. What about those who don't get that excited?

Maybe the words of Seth Godin, a go-to authority on branding, will help. He defines branding as

"a set of expectations, memories, stories, and relationships that—looked at together—account for
a consumer's decision to choose one product or
service over another. If the consumer doesn't pay
a premium, make a selection or spread the good
word, then no brand value exists for that consumer."[3] And, no brand value means no purchase—
which translates to no moo-lah.

A BRIEF **HISTORY.**

Have you ever wondered where
the term "branding" came from?
Believe it or not, it began as a simple solution for a person to differentiate his cattle from his neigh-
bors'. Each ranch needed their
own unique mark so ownership could be determined if their cattle somehow got mixed up with
the cattle from the ranch next door. The branding
mark needed to be simple, unique, and easy to
identify—all of which are traits commonly used today when developing brand identities and logos.

When goods were traded and shipped, the ship-
ping crates needed identifying marks so the
transporters (and recipients) knew what was inside. Over time, those marks became a symbol

of quality, not necessarily ownership. In the late 1800s a company could register a trademark to prevent others from creating "confusingly similar" trademarks. Confusingly similar is a term used in trademark law to determine if there is infringement on a product or service that looks, sounds, or feels too similar to another; thereby confusing the consumer into thinking it is related to the other brand in question. As a result, "brands" became valuable.[4] Fast forward to *Mad Men* romancing the whole idea of brand and all of a sudden, now brands were a "thing."

WHERE ARE THE **FISH?**

Does brand make sense yet? So far, you've learned that cows got a hot branding iron on the rump so they were easily identifiable for their owners and the word "brand" is difficult to understand. Let me break it down for you a bit further. Bottom line: you need to fish where there are fish.

Have you ever gone fishing? Believe it or not, I relate to it quite well since it has been a favorite activity for me and my son ever since he could hold a pole in his hand. Every summer, my parents and I would take Joey fishing. We would stay at cabins that had a pontoon boat and we would take it

out and fish all day. We would tootle around on those old rickety pontoons and sit for hours in the heat just waiting for a fish to nibble on our bait. If there were no nibbles, we had options: we either changed the bait or moved to a different location– and often times it was both! You see, certain fish prefer certain bait. So, depending on what you want to catch, you need to use that kind of bait. For instance, sunfish like worms, small and largemouth bass like leeches, walleye like minnows, and northern pike like daredevil lures. Different fish also like to swim at different depths, so you also need to know where the fish are swimming so they will bump into your bait, as well as knowing the areas of the lake where they like to hang out (such as near a sandbar, close to the weeds, or in deep, deep water). A mis-combination of location and bait means no fish on the line. And, because the fish swim and don't stay put, you need to be constantly pivoting in your seat to position yourself to where they are and give them the bait they want. It's a calculated game of "decide what I want to catch, give them the bait they want, then catch them." When my son and I go out, we have coolers and containers holding the various kinds of bait because to keep the bait alive you need certain conditions for each one, like moist soil (for worms) or ice (for leeches) or lake water (for minnows). We have giant tackle boxes with tackle segregated by fish category and we have supplies to take care of the caught fish until we can get to land and clean them properly. And, we don't keep every fish. There are rules on what (and how many) you can keep. And, if we don't follow the rules, we can get fined by the Department of Natural Resources. (Yes, there are fish police on the water who pay you the occasional visit to make sure you are doing the right things to protect the fish.)

So how does my son's summer fishing relate to brand? Think of the fish as your customers and the bait as your brand. You need to be where your customers are: online, in a retail store, or at an event (this is your location on the lake). You need to know what will draw them to you (bait) and you need to deliver it exactly how they want it (depth of line). If they see it, and they like it, they'll bite. But, what if they don't? Find yourself a brand strategist (a brand DNR if you will) and allow them to provide you with guidance and answers to help you garner attention.

WHAT IT'S **NOT.**

LOGO   BRAND

We've talked about what brand is, but what about what it's not? For many people, when you say "brand" they think "logo." But, a logo is only part of a brand. Brand is not just the logo, or the color palette, or the product or service, or the tone of voice. It's not just a business mission, or value, or vision. It's not marketing and it's not advertising. It's what your customer thinks of the whole of all of those parts. It's a feeling.

WHY IS BRAND SUCH A **BIG DEAL?**

Your brand is the single most important investment you can make in your business.

STEVE FORBES | FORBES EDITOR-IN-CHIEF

Brand is a promise and it's also how an audience "feels" about that promise. Think of it in terms of your familial relationships. When you are lied to by a member of your family or feel uncertain about their actions, how does that make you feel? Does it impact your trust in them short or long term? Will you question what they say or do for a period of time—or possibly indefinitely? If they hurt you in some way, will you be inclined to say, "Thank you. I'd like another, please"? No. You will retreat to a safer place—a place of certainty. A place where you can trust and where there will be truth. If your family member is a "brand," you want to feel assured she does what she says and that her response contributes to the family in a positive way. It's what we expect from brands: that they become a part of our family.

You've heard the term "tribe" before, I'm sure. When we align with a tribe, we induct ourselves into the tribal family. We believe their beliefs; we are perceived how they are perceived. This is the power of brand. With a strong resonating brand, you build a tribe of believers: believers in your product or service; believers in your business mission. And these believers will become raving fans and speak the good word about your wonderful brand. That's why brand is a big deal. Because if they—your potential customers—don't love you, they're probably indifferent or possibly worse: they may dislike you and share their feelings with others.

You see, you're a brand whether you do anything about it or not. How people "feel" about you and your business is your business. Don't you think you should influence those opinions—those feelings—when you can? If you do nothing, they form their own opinions. If those opinions are negative, those opinions can hurt you.

BRAND IS **TRUST BUILDING.**

Now that we've reviewed the definitions around brand, it's time to explore how to create a brand that builds trust with your customer. The secret is to build trust with customers through your brand the way you build a relationship with someone you care about. To create a long-lasting relationship you have to share the essence of who you are. To maintain that relationship, what you display on the outside (your brand promise) and how you behave (fulfilling that promise) must match. When we begin a relationship with someone on a first date and maintain it through decades, we mirror how successful brands meet, create, and retain loyal customers.

YOUR BRAND STARTS WITH A FIRST DATE.

Think back to a first date experience you've had. You probably considered everything from your clothes to the location and what kind of conversation you wanted to have, and all of your thoughts were intended to create an experience your date would want to repeat. Think of this first date scenario as reflective of the four steps in the branding process—four steps that, after the date, clinch a second date, and ideally a long-term relationship.

When you first meet the customer, consider the experience you want them to have that will compel them to reach out again.

1. Recognition: How do you want to be remembered? What emotion do you want to evoke? Think about the memory points of your first dates. Certain characteristics and mannerisms most likely stand out in your mind. Is your company's essence about tradition, modern minimalism, warmth, or are you avant-garde? Your brand design should clothe you in such a way that customers recognize who you are. What do you want their first impression of you to be?

2. Differentiation: How do you stand out from others? We all know the competition involved in dating, and it's no different when establishing your brand. How does your competition define itself? How do you talk about how you are different?

3. Confirmation: Once you're on the date, think about whether you are behaving consistently with the brand you're designing.

If your brand signals "modern and innovative," are you on the platforms where a tech-savvy customer would search for you? Can you be reached on multiple channels? How do you answer your phone? All these questions, in addition to the services you provide, must be consistent with the brand you are building. After all, if you want your date to think of you as social and connected, don't take him or her to a movie where you won't talk for two hours. Go somewhere filled with opportunities to interact.

4. Motivation: As your date winds down, have you set the tone for future interactions? Communicate how your professional goals and those of your customer—your date—intersect. Why would it be a good idea for him or her to court your business again?

Your relationship with your customer doesn't end as you part ways after the first date; you want a second date, right? What happens next will determine if that first date turns into a loyal fan.

1. Communication: What is your customer—your date—telling his or her friends? Audit the communication around your brand online and through surveys to ensure a consistent brand message and promise is getting through to your potential audience.

2. Consistency: Create a common experience time and again with everything you say and do. Have you ever been on a first date and felt they had a great sense of humor with a lighthearted view of the world and then, on the second date, they were a complaining disaster of a person filled with negativity? You say to yourself, "What?! Where is the person from date one?" If your brand is warm and traditional, are your offices? Are both your personal and professional Facebook accounts delivering the same message? Are you living your brand essence when you network? Does the design of your logo, website, and other marketing collateral visually match with what you say in words? If the answer to any of these questions is "no," there is some work to do on your brand consistency.

3. Focus: As you learn more about the person you are dating you'll begin to customize the experience. If you learn that he loves museums, you'll offer opportunities to go together. If she's a basketball fan, you could get tickets to a game. The same goes for your customers: first find out what their passions are, and then find a way to engage them with your brand.

4. Measurement: Did he have fun? Would she like to go out again? It's easy to measure the answers to these questions because we can ask them while dating. It's more complicated when measuring the results of your brand and marketing efforts. Was your message sticky? In other words, did it make sense and resonate with them? Is your offer converting? In other words, is your audience buying what you're selling? Without the answers to these questions it's difficult to adjust to the needs of your customers and make sure they have interpreted your brand the way you intended.

Are things clear as mud, or is brand starting to make sense? Before we get too far down the path, let's look at the elements of a brand.

BRAND **ARCHITECTURE.**

 Now that you have an understanding of what a brand is, let's chat about the components of a brand so you can actually start building one. I have an amazing mentor, Dave, who has the most giving spirit—and I happen to have him on speed dial. I'm happy to report even though he's a pretty big deal, he takes my calls. One of the little gems he has shared with me in the past is his definition of Brand Architecture; its core framework follows. I share this with you because if you understand the framework, you will have a better understanding of how to build your brand.

DAVE'S 6-POINT **BRAND ARCHITECTURE FRAMEWORK.**

1. Brand Promise: A simple expression of the brand benefit based upon a customer's expressed or latent need. Said another way, the experience is the brand. Therefore, what experience does your brand or company promise to the customer at every touch point?

2. Brand Positioning: A single-minded sentence that defines the idea the brand wants to own in the customers' and employees' minds. What does the brand do for people? How is it different from other brands and/or competitors in the category?

3. Brand Personality Traits: The character of the brand, how it acts in every situation. Another way to define these is to personify your brand. If your brand were a person at a cocktail party, how might he act or behave?

4. Reasons To Believe (RTBs): These are the functional benefits of the brand that often are focused on features or attributes of the product. Functional benefits aid in helping the consumer recognize a difference in the category—why they should believe in you instead of a competitor.

5. Reasons To Care (RTCs): These are the emotional benefits of the functional benefits discussed in point number four. With consumers often entering the purchase path first based on emotions, it is important to know why consumers should care about you. There are often intrinsic and extrinsic benefits—"intrinsic" being how we feel inside and "extrinsic" being how we are perceived on the outside.

6. Brand Values: The principles the brand holds as paramount.

A well-implemented brand communicates clearly who you are, what you do or sell, why you do it, and why people should care. The architecture of the brand is a necessary foundation to building a brand that is cohesive and resonates with its targeted audience. If you have this framework, you can build on it accordingly. You need to define your brand's identity—how it shows up through logo, color palette, and tone of voice. You need an overarching brand strategy to zero in on the pain your product or service solves for your ideal audience—and deliver a solution that will resonate in such a way that your customers rave about you and your brand. The brand promise is important because your audience needs to believe in you and your mission for how you plan to change the world. And, then there are brand extensions. A brand extension is leveraging your well-known brand name in one category to launch a new product or service in another category. Let's use a Starbucks example. They make coffee, so by adding coffee makers to their product suite that would be a brand extension. Brand extensions come into play when you find yourself with a need to expand upon your offerings. How will they work in conjunction with the main brand? Will they be brought under the umbrella of what exists or will there be micro-brands?

An example of a micro brand would be Xbox; which is a micro-brand of Microsoft. Xbox isn't a sub-brand; it's an independent brand that happens to belong to Microsoft. See the difference?

Coming up with a vetted brand architecture includes consideration of all of these and more. You'll need to think of your brand's tone of voice and word usage, what the brand's shtick is, and what it will be known for. You'll need to determine how you will position yourself and your brand against the competition and figure out how "specifically" you are different than and better than them—and whether or not you need a tagline to make messaging clearer. Having a brand architecture defined and built will get you well on your way to sales without having to be "salesy."

BRAND VS. PRODUCT.

So what's the difference between a brand and a product?

Let's use Starbucks as our example for this discussion. Coffee is the product. Starbucks is the brand. What's the difference? Emotion. You like coffee. You might even love it. (I know I do.) But what coffee brand do you prefer and, more importantly, why do you prefer it? Is it home grown (meaning only

23

available in your area, so you support your community) or is the brand socially conscious—giving back one cup at a time? Do you like them because they put your name on the cup? Do they roast the beans right there in front of you? Notice I have not mentioned anything about the coffee itself—how it functions or how it tastes.

I like coffee for a variety of reasons. The "product" appeal is that there is caffeine that helps me produce at full throttle in the morning regardless of how early I wake up. I like the routine of brewing, smelling its aroma, and holding the warm mug in my hand. The "brand" appeal is when I purchase coffee when I'm out and about. The convenience in Starbucks locations and how I am treated from the time I walk through the door to the time I leave fulfills a want. Technically, I could get my coffee anywhere, but I choose a specific brand because of the "brand."

Having a **strong brand** beats the heck out of selling. Do you think Oprah had to go around and convince people to be a guest on her show?

KELLY LUCENTE

SO **WHAT?**

So, how does defining your brand make you moo-lah? Brand building is probably not a line item on your Profit and Loss Statement (P&L), but it should be because your profit will definitely increase based upon the strength of your brand.

1. If you have a strong brand value, your customer is willing to pay more for your product or service.

Consider this scenario:

Kellogg School of Management conducted a study with some of their MBA students. The professor asked the first group of students what they would expect to pay for a pair of good-quality, 18-karat gold earrings. He asked a second group how much they would pay for the same product, but added the words "from Tiffany." He asked a third group the same question, but changed "from Tiffany" to "from Wal-Mart." The results were striking. The average price for the unbranded earrings was $550. With Tiffany branding, the average price increased to $873, a jump of almost 60%—an increase due solely to the addition of the brand name. With the Wal-Mart branding, the price expectation fell to just $81, a decline of 85% from the unbranded example and a decline of 91% from the Tiffany brand.[5] There is something very important to be learned from this example. Not only does the power of brand shape a buyer's perception, "good" quality means something entirely different between brands depending on their "perceived" value.

WALMART **UNBRANDED** **TIFFANY & CO.**

$81 $550 $873

2. If you have a strong brand—one that is perceived as an industry leader—you can avoid becoming a commodity.

If your product or service is just like everyone else's, then you are a commodity and competition will become a real-time issue. In that case, we compete solely on price and that drives margins down. How? By forcing us to discount or offer "free" incentives to get our customers to consider us. People don't buy a BMW or a VW Beetle solely based upon their difference in price. Even though they are both German-made automobiles and both get us from point A to point B, the drivers of each are very different from one another. These vehicles offer us very different features, as well as vastly different brand impressions. Can you picture the driver of each in your mind? Which one are you?

3. The strongest brands have the biggest competitive advantage.

Think about Crocs. They're the premier brand in their space, commanding 90% of the springy-soled, plastic clog market. There have been numerous other similar products that have come on the scene trying to grab hold of this particular consumer shoe fetish, but none have been as successful. Unless you have a strong IP strategy ("intellectual property": think copyright; think trademark; think patent), you will have competition, so being the frontrunner in every possible way will be paramount. Your brand awareness is especially important because if you are at the top of a consumer's mind, you will be the go-to for consideration.

CLOSING THE **LOOP.**

I know we covered a lot in this first chapter; how-ever, it was necessary to give you a clear under-standing of brand so you know what to do with it in the following chapters. For those of you who do better with soundbites, listed below are the pivotal takeaways from this chapter and you will find these "brand bits" at the end of every chapter throughout the book.

BRAND BITS.

- Brands answer the "who," "what," "how," and most importantly, the "why."

- Branding is a they game.

- Branding works for or against you. It never stays static.

- Brands make you "feel."

- No brand value = No moo-lah.

- Brand is not a logo. It's the sum of its parts.

- Brand is a promise.

- Details mean everything.

- Look at your brand holistically.

- Brand = Trust. Trust = Moo-lah.

CHAPTER **TWO**

ARE YOU IN, OR ARE YOU OPTIONAL?

"Are you in or are you optional?" is the very first thing I ask someone who expresses interest in working with me. I know it sounds a bit off putting, but it's necessary because my advice will be commensurate with the answer I receive from the person I'm asking. And, based upon the length of the answer, I assess how many times I'm going to hear "but" while we are doing the tasks necessary to launch. I disdain the word "but," to be honest. To me, "but" is like fingernails on a chalkboard because it holds us back from getting the work done and this entire chapter is about *the work*.

The work is the foundation of every process. Imagine you are building a house. You wouldn't jump right to putting on a roof if you didn't have walls to hold it up. You wouldn't put up those walls without a foundation to hold them in place, since the foundation is the stability of the structure. The foundation also has to support the entire weight of the building and everything that's inside it. A small building needs a small foundation, but a big building needs a larger foundation. The stronger the foundation, the taller the structure can be. If you have a weak foundation, the structure is vulnerable to instability, which could cause it to fall down or topple onto itself. One of the most famous examples of this metaphor is the Leaning Tower of Pisa in Italy. It was built on a weak foundation (only three meters thick) and, as a result, has been leaning an additional .05 inches per year.[6] (Having spent almost two decades associated with the home building industry, going to Italy to walk through that tower is definitely on my bucket list.) That being said, the tower is unstable and could fall over at any time for a variety of reasons. Only time will tell. As much positive attention as the Leaning Tower of Pisa gets, you don't want your business to be known for the fact that it could collapse at any moment. You need a strong foundation if you want it to pass the tests of time because, as your business grows and evolves, there will be plenty of metaphorically high winds and unstable ground trying to knock your business over.

IT'S IN THE **EYES,** OR IN THE **SIGHS.**

WARNING: If at any point during this chapter you find yourself rolling your eyes or sighing or saying, "Oh heck, no!" out loud, close the book and gift it to a friend. I'm serious. Even though the following chapters are WAY more fun, they are pointless if you don't digest— then do—what's on the next several pages.

NOT FOR THE FAINT OF HEART.

There was a period of time when my son Joey thought he wanted to be a chef–so much so I added an 800-square-foot kitchen addition onto our house to give him the space necessary to really hone his culinary skills. Each Christmas and birthday he received the latest cooking gadgets, which included an amazing set of chef's knives. You can imagine how excited he was as an eager sixth grader to enthusiastically "create" in the kitchen. On one particular day, I was sitting at the kitchen island watching him chop with those very fancy, very sharp knives. He was using a rapid technique I can't even define, although I've seen it a bunch of times on The Food Network, and trying to emulate the technique. I told him to slow down, and told him once I had a close encounter between my finger and a knife and it took forever to heal. He assured me he knew what he was doing and, sure enough, the minute he finished his sentence he sliced his finger wide open. He grabbed his hand with such force he splattered blood on the ceiling of our brand-new kitchen. Clearly, it wouldn't have done me any good to have said, "I told you so." Instead, I rushed to his aid and we stopped the bleeding and bandaged him up, and I finished the chopping.

Many years later, those little droplets of blood are

still visible on the ceiling and are a reminder to both of us that when I give him advice, I'm not doing it to be controlling or to be a nag—I'm sharing insight from the learnings of my past. I've walked a mile or two in his shoes and it's through my own stumbles that I can bring a level of knowledge to him with the hope that he can avoid a few along the way. Now when he pushes back, I just point to the ceiling. He gets the message.

I know this is easier said than done, to accept someone's advice blindly. We all need to walk our own paths and take our own journeys, but as it pertains to branding—and the pitfalls of your business—sometimes learning those lessons is really expensive. I'm trying to help you avoid any expense that could be avoided. You see, I've had the pitfalls. I've fallen on my face in business.

I've had to throw in the towel and give up something I felt extremely passionate about—something I loved. I've already failed for you, so I know—really know—what to do and what to avoid. This book may come off harsh (especially this chapter), but believe me when I say there's really no option for you but to do the work.

I've seen branding done well and I've seen it done poorly—so poorly that I've watched business owners burn through their savings, their children's future educations, and their financial resources to the point where they had nothing left to sacrifice trying to figure it all out. I've seen brand failure. I've experienced it personally and I've watched friends and clients go through it. It's not pretty. For those who are parents, you want what's best for your children. You want to help them avoid as much pain as possible. That's what I'm going to try and do for you with **MOO-LAH-GY.** You'll wind up doing the work one way or another with or without my help. Those who avoid the foundational "work" will pay for it as it rears its ugly head down the road in the form of re-work. I know this because I see it happening every day. This book is your opportunity to step around some of those yucky moments in business. So what do you think? Shall we get to work?

THE **WIDGET.**

Do you know what you sell? Your "widget?" I know that sounds like a really silly question, but it's one you should ask yourself from time to time. How many of you have attended a networking event and been asked "So, what do you do?" What does your answer sound like? Are you happy with it? Is who you are and what you sell crystal clear? If not, I'd suggest getting clearer. Without the widget, the thing you sell, the reason you are in business, and being clear, how do you expect your audience to buy? If what you're saying doesn't make sense to you, it certainly won't make sense to the person you're speaking to.

In order to make a buying decision, dots must connect—starting with the widget. We cover connecting the dots in chapter 5, but for now just know people *want* to understand what you're selling. Make it easy for them. Have you ever asked someone what they do and they go on and on for sometimes what feels like ten minutes and, when they pause and smile at you as if they've just presented the best college dissertation, you still don't know what they do? When I hear this, I say, "I'm sorry, what do you do?" And they look at me in total disbelief of my inability to "get it." Some are even offended. I've watched these same people go on and on and on to the point where the listener's eyes roll back into their head, but they keep going on and on.

Here's the thing: if you are clear on what you do and what you sell, you will be able to communicate it in a way that allows the listener to "get it" as well. If they get it, they'll probably inquire more, because you've nailed your explanation and it will be a refreshing change to those who struggle to understand the masses' explanations. You might even get a high-five. Here's an example of the *best* explanation I've ever heard. It was so good, I almost cried.

I met a young fellow at an entrepreneur's event. He greeted me. "Hi, I'm Buddy." I asked him what he did and he said, "I make peanut butter." Yep. Exactly. I went to his website and that is exactly what he does. What can we learn from this? You don't have to over complicate the explanation. Simply understand what your widget is (in Buddy's case, it was making peanut butter) and state it. You can always define more (like why you do what you do and why that particular widget) as your conversation naturally evolves.

Bottom line is what I like to call the **Three Cs: Connecting Dots = Clarity = Close.**

Now that you know what you sell and the difference between a brand and a product, let's build.

THE **FOUNDATION.**

Not everyone goes into business because they love *running* a business. Entrepreneurs I know have started their own companies because they love cooking, enjoy teaching people about nutrition, like building online communities, or had a life-changing experience. I receive multiple calls every day from people who have a business idea they want to birth from a passion they have. I love to hear their stories of how they arrived at their sketch on the napkin because it's in the backstory where the business plan begins. Some calls come from people who already have established businesses, but they are in a growth or transition stage and need some guidance to scale. Whatever your stage of business, the foundational process is invaluable. But for the purpose of this section of the book, let's assume you are starting from the beginning—or pretty close to the beginning. The beginning is where we formulate our plan.

It's helpful to think of planning in four stages. First, you'll define your mission and your brand message. The second step is to assess the industry, your place in it, and who your customers and competitors are. Third, how you are different and why your customer cares is covered in the differentiation stage. And finally, you'll focus on setting your goals and objectives so all the work you've done doesn't stop cold. With all four, you'll have a plan to carry your business forward.

DEFINE.

WHO DO YO U	**WHAT** DO YOU	**WHY** CHOOSE
SERVE?	**OFFER?**	**YOU?**
TARGET	CONTRIBUTION	VALUE

Business moves fast; sometimes it moves so quickly there is little time to think, let alone define what and why we do what we do. We simply *do*. Taking the time to define your business mission and brand has benefits that will compel you to slow down and take the time to define your purpose. The reason this is so important is if you don't have a clear understanding of what you do, you can't expect your customer to understand. I know we talked a bit about this when we were discussing our widget, but how do we come up with the explanation to define it? We start with a mission statement. To begin, let's take a peek at some of the benefits of a mission statement.

A mission statement:

1. Spells out a company's "reason for existing" for both internal stakeholders and customers.
2. Allows you to thoughtfully articulate the value you provide to a select target market.
3. Guides decision-making and strategy so you're not trying to do everything at once.

Without a written mission statement, business owners struggle to call out the most compelling benefits of the products and services they provide. A wonderful friend and client of mine, Paula, the CEO (Chief *Experience* Officer) of Hotelements, whose audience segments included both B2B (business to business) and B2C (business to customer) is a perfect example of how coming up with a mission statement can make all the difference in messaging and positioning. The company was struggling to describe how a deep-seated passion for boutique hotels could become an opportunity for today's hotel guests (homeowners) to bring a hotel's signature elements or "hotelements" home—as well as consulting with boutique hotels on how to expand and enhance the guest experience before, during, and after a guest checks out. Speaking to two different audiences with one voice was not easy. After extensive work on her mission statement, she was able to describe her benefits in web copy and marketing collateral with ease to *both* audiences and create messaging to clearly communicate the value (and need) of the business.

So, what is a mission statement?

MISSION STATEMENT

A statement that captures **why** your business exists.
Why does your business do what it does?
Who is it for? And, **why** should anyone care?

In other words, **"So What?"**

I find the best mission statements don't exceed a few sentences. The goal is to encapsulate what you do, how you do it, who you do it for, and the value you bring—all in one succinct statement. Let's take a look at Twitter's mission statement.

 *To give everyone the power to create and share ideas and information instantly, without barriers.*

So what does that mean? It means anyone can join and enjoy Twitter. There are no requirements for entry and you can share your ideas, opinions, and information in real time without censorship. Brilliant! Clean, clear, and to the point.

Once you're solid on your mission statement, you need to turn it into a value proposition (or a unique selling proposition) which gets communicated outwardly to your target audience. The ideal value proposition uses words and phrases that resonate with your customer and answer the question of "What's in it for them?" It needs to speak their language, address their pain, and provide a solution.

AT ITS CORE, A **VALUE PROPOSITION** IS A STATEMENT THAT **COMMUNICATES** THE **VALUE** OF **WHAT** YOU DO, **FOR** WHOM, AND **WHY** THEY CARE.

Let's use Twitter again as our example. If I were creating a value proposition for them based upon their mission statement, it would sound something like this:

We believe in a voice being heard—in real time—in 140 characters or less. We believe in brevity and communication in the purest sense of the word giving everyone freedom of expression with an international reach.

A value proposition allows you to express three things:

> **1.** How your business solves your customer's problems (relevancy).
> **2.** What your specific benefits (specific values) are.
> **3.** Why your ideal customer should buy from you and not your competitor.

ASSESS.

I recently mentored a young team chosen as semifinalists in an entrepreneurship program that offers the winners seed moo-lah (if they win) to apply to the growth of their business. The team is required to submit a business plan that includes a mission statement and value proposition, and by

the time I was assigned as their mentor, they had already gone down the path of designing packaging, launching social media, and so forth—all without a foundation. They were introducing a new hard cider to the market place and had thousands of cans in production.

Our task was to create a business plan and an investor pitch, neither of which they had in place. The first thing I asked them was "Who are you?" They couldn't answer me. I shared with them that if they didn't know who they were and what they stood for as a company, they could not expect their customers to know. They shared with me, however, that they were very clear on who their buyer demographic was: millennial women. I asked them what they knew about their demographic. They didn't know much. I asked them what their customers' buying preferences were, where they hung out, and whether or not they even preferred hard cider over other alcoholic beverages. They couldn't answer. This disconnect between execution and planning created an interesting challenge because after doing "the work," they realized they had, in fact, done things a bit backward. Re-work is not your ideal scenario, because it leaves doubt in your buyer's mind. (I'm happy to report these motivated business owners pushed through the pain and now have their hard cider in multiple retail locations.)

WHERE ARE YOU NOW?

You might have heard about a "SWOT" analysis, but have you ever created one? SWOT analyses can be used for everything from making a decision on where to go to college, to whether to outsource work in your business, or how to set your strategic plans. You need to perform a SWOT to get the lay of the land. It is a way to compare yourself against the competition in four specific areas to determine your differentiators and build a brand to support the business mission. A SWOT analysis is like a snapshot of a moment in time. To stay on top of trends in your industry, it's a great practice to use this tool with your employees—or as a solopreneur—on a regular basis.

WHAT DOES SWOT STAND FOR?

S = Strengths

These are internal factors in your business that are strong and help you reach your goals. Things like the experience on your marketing team, your brand's recognition, market share, strong customer relationships, etc., are on this list. These internal factors are the ones you can control.

W = Weaknesses

Weaknesses are internal factors within the company's control. I know it's hard to imagine we'd allow weaknesses, but that's not the spirit of this section. There's always room for improvement. Is there a particular type of customer you're having trouble serving? Are you finding it a challenge to hire the right people? How are your cash reserves? The best source for determining your weaknesses comes from your customer service data. What are people asking your business to improve and why?

O = Opportunities

Too often, small business owners are internally focused. The SWOT tool prods us to look at the trends in our external environment, and the trends that offer potential for business growth are listed in this Opportunities section. Here you'd list trends like a boom in online promotions, niche publications for marketing, a competitor exiting the market, or changes in consumer preferences that lean in your company's direction. As a business owner, if you can't control the factor, yet it helps you, this is where to put it.

T = Threats

The opposite of opportunities are trends in the industry that hinder your company's growth. If spending on corporate training is trending down and you're a professional speaker, that's a threat. Consider trends in demographics, buyer preferences, competition, marketing platforms, and the economy. Remember to include external factors and those you can't control, but will impact the functioning of your business in the short and long term.

To bring a SWOT analysis to life, on the opposite page I'll show you the one I used when I created a children's educational product called "Bye Bye Monster" (BBM). This product (a complete bedtime solution to help children ages 4-12 years who struggled with nighttime fear) aided the children by empowering them to overcome those fears on their own through imaginative play, so they could successfully sleep through the night. Ideally in your SWOT analysis, you'll want three to four items to appear in each panel of the analysis.

Does the idea of a SWOT analysis make more sense now that you've seen an example? I would encourage you to give it a try and create one based upon what you know right now about your business. Remember, you can always add to and/or modify it as you go.

STRENGTHS
3-5 STRENGTHS

- BBM offers a complete bedtime solution covering all three bases (comfort, voice, protection) and the majority of the competition is singularly focused only addressing one or two areas when, in fact, the experts state all three must be addressed to be effective.

- Strong branding is present throughout because of the partnership between Tim Brazier (professional illustrator) and Re-Tool Marketing.

- Strong customer feedback on proof of concept. Social proof is showing the product is effective and is working.

WEAKNESSES
3-5 WEAKNESSES

- Because the product is all-natural, it only has a 3-4 year shelf life which makes it difficult to carry enough overhead to keep price point low.

- Small batch production will inhibit large orders from big box retailers or home shopping networks.

- The all-natural room spray cannot be patented; thus, risk for duplication or knock offs coming to market without any recourse.

- Rapid expansion might cripple the business without strong leadership.

OPPORTUNITIES
3-5 OPPORTUNITIES

- 73% of children between the ages of 3-12 struggle with nighttime fear which equates to 26 million children and the number is growing at an annual increase of 2.3%.

- Corporate tie-ins with bed manufacturers as well as children's bedding products as a companion product partner are viable as incentive partnerships with companies such as Parent Magazine and Jenny McCarthy's Generation Rescue autism foundation.

- With the surge of all things "healthier", the market opportunity is growing to include better food options as well as cosmetics and cleaners. BBM fits the trend.

THREATS
3-5 THREATS

- CPSIA rules and regulations do not know how to categorize the spray portion of the 3-part set as it isn't technically a "toy" and all toys need screening, but if categorized as a fragrance, it does not need testing.

- A Hasbro or Mattel could easily ramp up and scale a competitive product due to their size and resources.

- The possibility of a lawsuit from an allergic reaction to one of the essential oils is a concern.

- Small competitive players can easily enter the market at a lower price point by introducing a spray only.

WHO IS YOUR CUSTOMER?

When I ask the question "Who is your customer?" the answer is almost unanimously "everyone"—but that isn't possible, even if you are Coca-Cola. Even though Coca-Cola is one of the most recognized brands in the world, it markets to specific buyer demographics.

At some point you'll fall into the trap of wanting to reach everyone with your offer. Don't worry, we've all been there, trying to be all things to all people. For example, McDonald's doesn't target "everyone who's hungry," they simply target demographics based upon menu, location, convenience, and price—so you shouldn't think a customer who likes widgets will want to buy everyone's widgets. Their motivation regarding a widget is very specific. Does this particular widget solve their problem? And, what the problem is varies for everyone. Targeting your customer into one or more personas, or profiles, will help you better communicate and market to the people who value and need what you provide. Because focused targeting will help you hone in on your market, it will save you moo-lah on the front end and make you moo-lah on the back end.

> Don't find **customers** for your products, find **products** for your customers.
>
> **SETH GODIN**

Often times, a product or service is built based on a personal need or a passion to create it without giving consideration to whether there is an audience who actually wants it. Doesn't that sound a little backward? It is. You need to determine if there is a customer base interested enough to buy what you're selling—and who are willing to tell all of their friends to do the same. So how do you determine if that audience exists? Research. Define your target audience and then speak to them. Don't freak out. Research is not a four-letter word. It can actually be quite fun. Let me show you how.

As I mentioned, one of the "fun" things you can do is develop "personas" for your customer base. Personas are descriptions of your ideal buyer based upon certain criteria. You will be surprised how helpful it will be to give your customer(s) a persona. It will be so much easier to speak and sell to them. Before developing your customer personas, first narrow down your customers by target. You can start with broad strokes like the following categories:

> **1.** Demographics are the statistical data the census bureau collects about the population such as age, gender, income, education, etc. This category is overemphasized, so don't stop here.

> **2.** Geographic segmentation involves where your target lives, but you need to go beyond their country or even state. Think about factors such as "urban vs. rural." It might be helpful to drill down to their ZIP code. Your goal is to get to know your customers—this includes where they live and work.

> **3.** Psychographic segment analysis explores consumer attitudes, aspirations, interests, beliefs, and personality. What do your consumers read? Are they more

likely to be on LinkedIn or Facebook? What groups do they belong to? What are their favorite movies, TV shows, or music? The more you know about your customer the better you'll be able to anticipate their needs.

4. Consumption behavior is important to study once you've secured some customers. Who buys product A versus product B? Why? What is the profile of your retainer customer vs. the once-a-year "Quick, I need your help!" customer?

If you're thinking you don't have the time to figure this all out—and again, I've been there—I'm telling you there isn't time not to do it. Remember the example of the company selling hard cider and their painful lesson? Well, I've got a million of those stories. Knowing your customer helps you sell to your customer in a way that's personal and relevant. Consumers are so savvy today that generic messages just aren't going to cut the mustard.

Let me share a customer persona with you.

PERSONA EXAMPLE.

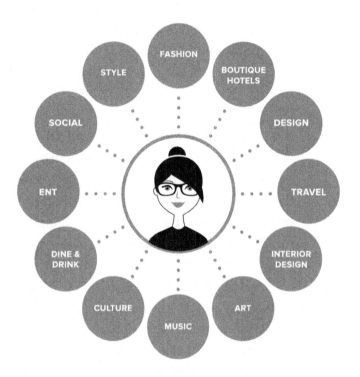

Remember our hotel company example from earlier? One of the beautiful things about the CEO of that business is that she absolutely knows what her client persona looks like. She even created a visual to refer to while she built the infrastructure of her business, as well as all messaging and positioning work. Everything she "built" was in the spirit of a persona she developed named "Chloe" and what Chloe would want. She shared with me how immensely helpful it was to put herself in the shoes of

Chloe as she created products and services to sell to her audience. She even took it a step further and her male ("Chase") and female ("Chloe") personas are listed on her website.

Chloe's description looks like this:

> *"Chloe is a 32 year old marketing director born in New York, but currently living in Portland, Oregon. She exemplifies the new 'creative' traveler.*
>
> *"Educated on the sunny West Coast, Chloe became an avid outdoors gal with a large sense of adventure. She now holds an executive position at a large athletics company in the Pacific Northwest and spends half her time traveling to their other offices across the globe.*
>
> *"Chloe is an eclectic spirit, loves her after work dance club as much as she appreciates the boardroom. She relies heavily on her 'mobile' device and while she prefers posting on her Pinterest page, it's not unusual to see a few tweets and Facebook posts documenting her daily experiences.*

"Chloe's on the forefront of fashion, design, art and technology and can effortlessly blend a T-Shirt from Zara with a skirt from Tory Burch. She is comfortable with her look and style and is always craving an outlet for self-expression. She loves staying in boutique hotels and while she is often busy working in the communal spaces, [she] loves knowing there are like-minded individuals close by.

"Chloe likes to check out the local music scene and shopping when she can and enjoys connecting and sharing her experiences with her close friends when she returns home."

Can you picture Chloe in your mind? Have you started to formulate your own customer personas? Give it a try and remember nothing is absolute. Allow these personas to be a bit fluid, meaning that you can add to them and change them as needed as your business grows and evolves.

WHO ARE YOUR COMPETITORS?

Ah, competition; rare is the business which truly doesn't have any; however, many small businesses operate as if they have none. When did you last look at your competitors' websites? How about their social media pages and strategies? Can you summarize their strengths and weaknesses? If your answer to any of these questions is a "no," you'll find this next section particularly helpful.

I recently had a client hire me to re-Brand their ten-year-old wealth management firm. As part of the re-Brand, we included a competitive analysis to get a feel for where they ranked in comparison to others in their industry and location. Through our work, we not only discovered where there was significant opportunity for growth, but which competition was ahead in market share, or behind them, respectively. Our research also gave them a sense of certainty around the re-Brand direction I was suggesting because the advice was no longer subjective, but based upon observable proof. The re-Brand meant everything would change from logo design to how they spoke to clients, so they needed confidence in my research if they were to move forward with my recommendations.

So how do you measure competition against your own business? By completing a competitive analysis. Completing a competitive analysis involves four parts: identifying your competitors, gathering competitive information, analyzing the information, and determining your competitive position. Let's look at each in turn.

1. Identifying your top three competitors.

When you identify these competitors think about your entire line of products and services. What niches do you fit into? Are there substitutes for your products or services? Does your competition offer something similar, or better in comparison?

Let's look at the cereal market, one of my all-time favorite industries to look at because they are so fiercely competitive. As you can see from this chart, there is quite a bit of competition in the space.[7] They are competing against each other for shelf space in supermarkets—and for market share. So, how do they gain market share (and increase sales)? They need to consider the competitor that is one stage bigger than they are at the time—and the one that is one stage smaller. They need to review each one to see if the competitors are trying to reach the same target market, or if they are going after different audiences. You need to ask yourself similar questions and perform the same research in order to narrow your list of competitors down to three. You could compare against more, but why complicate things? Three will suffice.

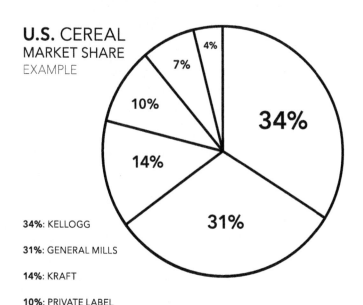

U.S. CEREAL
MARKET SHARE
EXAMPLE

34%: KELLOGG

31%: GENERAL MILLS

14%: KRAFT

10%: PRIVATE LABEL

7%: PEPSICO (QUAKER)

4%: OTHER

2. Gathering competitive information.

The web will be your best friend for this process, but don't discount offline methods such as focus groups or "secret shops." There is a lot you can glean from a room full of people who have had exposure to your competition that can help you to get an understanding of their experiences. When I was in the homebuilding industry, I would perform secret shops on the competition by going in and acting as if I was interested in purchasing a home so I could observe their processes and closing skills. I would take that information back to my builder and pivot (if necessary) using the real-time research by implementing appropriate changes to my own sales team.

You might want to set up a table in a Microsoft Word or Google document to help organize your information. (I'm a visual learner, so a table works great for me.) Then, you can brainstorm what you want to compare before you begin. For example, if I'm at the stage of branding a business, I'll pay attention to brand promise, colors, style, tone, etc. If I'm building a business with a focus on marketing, I'll add my competitor's special offers, social media streams, benefits and features, hours of operation, and so on. It's easy to get overwhelmed, which is why I suggest brainstorming *what you want to learn before you dive in*. You can find yourself on a wild goose chase if you're not careful, so organization is important.

3. Analyze the information.

I'll show you a way to make comparisons quickly and easily. You'll need the information you've gathered from your SWOT analysis, as well as the notes on your customers and your competitors, to pull it altogether. When you're ready, you can use a table like the one found on the next page.

CUSTOMER PERSONA/DESCRIPTION

Anthony: Savvy small business owner looking for unique swag for multiple events that speak to his brand. *(Enter the persona/description here to keep the customer at the core of your decision-making.)*

	STRENGTHS	WEAKNESSES
MY BUSINESS	• Highly personalized. • All three partners have over 10 years corporate experience. • Three-day turnaround on orders.	• Branding is unclear. • Website design does not match brand. • Little name recognition in local market.
COMPETITOR A	• Has largest portion of market share. • Offers extensive line. • Greatest name recognition.	• Contract businesses are not receiving responsive service. • Customers feel like a number. • Prices have been increasing.
COMPETITOR B	• Fast moving. • Web based. • Lower price due to automation.	• Tech still new - has had some glitches. • Employees relatively inexperienced. • No local roots.
COMPETITOR C	• Serves niche successfully. • Highly specialized employees. • New product lines added every year.	• Little/no name recognition outside of industry. • New product inconsistent with brand. • Slower to ship orders.

4. Determine your competitive position.

Perhaps your mission includes treating each customer as if he or she is the only one, providing service or products to them quickly, and offering each customer a wealth of experience. (Keep in mind I wrote the example on the left to show you the concept in a neat and tidy package.) Often the position you'll want to take won't be so cut and dried, but can give you a starting point. Armed with your analysis, you can make the decisions that allow you to speak to your potential customers with relevance and confidence.

That's it! That's a competitive analysis. Simple, straightforward, and to the point—and that is the point. Backing up your decisions with industry research doesn't have to be complicated, but it does need to get done. Why? So you can take the next steps in your planning with confidence. And, who doesn't love a little swagger?

DIFFERENTIATE.

You've done the hard work to truly understand where you fit in the industry and you've identified the value you bring. Now, we get to talk about what makes you special. Identifying differentiators is one of the favorite parts of my job. I love coming up with unique ways to differentiate my clients from the competition and position my clients in a favorable light.

The objective with differentiation is uncovering what is special about a product or service in such a way that it's memorable and preferable. Positioning is a key ingredient to the branding process and is the single most overlooked component from a management point of view. Believe it or not, we are positioning all the time. Think about it: you're invited to a party at someone's home. It's an evening event and kids are invited. You walk into the house and what do you do? Do you readily step into ongoing conversations with the adults, or do you grab a seat over by the kids and join in on a game on the PS4? Do you bring a dish to share or show up empty-handed? Are you dressed in a formal gown or did you come straight from the gym and didn't bother to change—or shower? Do you bring a bottle of tequila and suggest everyone do shots or do you slowly sip on the house wine? Each example—good, bad, or otherwise—is positioning.

Positioning creates perception, and perception, in many cases, creates people's reality. It's very difficult to change a first impression. Remember: people need to put things in boxes. This includes you, your business, your product, and your service. These "boxes" help others decide how they feel about any and all of the items I've just mentioned (including you). They form an opinion—positive or negative—so wouldn't it be beneficial to help steer that opinion?

Have you ever been judged based upon your appearance? Any time I've ever needed to return something to a store and I've misplaced my receipt, I "dress for it." I put on a suit and walk in like I'm an important business person instead of heading over in my sweats after the gym. I've actually tested my theory on attire impacting service. When I'm wearing my suit I'm positioned from a place of authority and as a result, when I speak, the customer service personnel listen. I believe the differentiation lies in the suit, and the attitude while I'm in the suit. Once I needed to swing by Tiffany &

Co. to pick up a gift for a friend and I was wearing casual clothes. The security guard watched me the entire time I was in the store and I felt extremely uncomfortable. It felt as though I didn't deserve to be in there. Conversely, during another trip to the same store after an event in which I spoke, I felt like I was treated very differently. I was dressed in a business suit and was pleasantly greeted by security as well as the staff behind the counter. Each scenario was an entirely different experience all due to my attire.

SAINT PAUL

I grew up in St. Paul, Minnesota. For those who are familiar with the Twin Cities, you know that if you grew up in St. Paul (the east side of the Mississippi river), you generally don't cross to the west side of the river (Minneapolis) or vice versa. Even as an adult, I lived in a St. Paul suburb until I had my son, Joey. He attended kindergarten and first grade in the suburb where I lived and, in first grade, was pulled out of class to attend accelerated reading and math, but he would come home crying that he missed snack and didn't get to be in class with his friends. Since I had a new issue on the table, I decided to look at things from a long-term perspective. If I kept him in his current school, he would continue to be pulled out of class, which was not something I wanted for him. So what were my options? I could put him in a private school, but after doing the research decided that did not fit with our lifestyle or what I wanted for him. I wanted him to be in the same category as the kids who are considered for academic achievement opportunities, but were in the public sector (positioning). Further consideration brought my attention to a high school—across the river on the Minneapolis side of the river. The high school was continually ranked in the top three schools in the Twin Cities in student performance year after year, so I knew my son would be challenged. I also learned that many of the school's students received college scholarships because of their elevated test scores. The perception of the district was one of prestige and respect. I knew if I put my son into that district he would have a very good chance of positioning himself for a college of his choice. So I decided to uproot us and move. It wound up being the right choice because I am happy to report my son entered the Carlson School of Management at the University of Minnesota, one of the top-ranked business schools in the nation with forty-six credits under his belt. Without an entrance exam, he was accepted off his application. There is no doubt my son deserved to be at Carlson due to his merits and hard work, but I believe his having attended the school district he did sincerely helped when the University of Minnesota was making their student selections. That's positioning.

So how does my son's story apply to business? Take M&M candies for example. M&Ms were created based upon their main differentiator. The candy-coated shell was intended to prevent the chocolate from melting during the summer months when there was no air conditioning, because "regular" chocolate sales went down during the summer. Their main differentiator is reflected in their slogan: "Melts in your mouth, not in your hand" which is one of the "most liked" and well known advertising slogans of all time.[8] Did you know M&Ms were exclusively sold to American soldiers during WWII as part of their rations? It wasn't until after the war the popular candy was made available to the general public.[9] The product had a differentiator (the ability to not melt until being eaten) that met a consumer need they were positioned to fill.

Ask yourself how you stand out from the crowd. How do you plan to stay relevant? As you work with your team to discover your differentiators in-depth, there are three areas where you can concentrate your brainstorming:

Process Capabilities: What processes do you have that allow you to meet the needs of your customers in a way only your business can? Best Buy has its Geek Squad who can come to you (or you to them) for repairs on the products you purchase.

Business Attributes: What products, services, features, and benefits does your business provide that appeal specifically to your ideal customer? How do you deliver these attributes better than your competition? Ever been in an Apple store or own any of their products? There have been a double-digit number of employees working in the store each and every time I've gone, so there's rarely ever a waiting period. They have been very prompt in service and have issued resolution that makes sense for me. Anytime I've ever purchased equipment, set up time and effort has been at a minimum. It feels very turn-key in comparison to other similar products I've purchased in the past. Apple products feel more fluid. Their products are designed for workflow, so as a creative, Apple is perfect for my team and me.

General Criteria: How are you able to meet and exceed your buyers' needs for price, value, quality, and speed? Have you ever made a purchase from Zappos? The are known for price, value, quality, customer service, and especially speed. Speaking to customer service, I recently had a conversation with someone referring to Zappos' customer service. He told a story about how a woman lost her husband, so she was returning his unworn shoes. She received flowers in the mail with Zappos' condolences. Keep in mind these general criteria are the easiest differentiators for your competition to copy, so lean on the other categories before this one—unless you can nail them all in one fell swoop like Zappos.

Still not sure what to consider for differentiators? Here are some ideas:

- Service Quality
- Product Feature(s)
- Premium Offering(s)

- Convenience
- Delivery Speed
- Expertise
- Warranty
- Social Consciousness

PLAN.

> **"**
> A **GOAL** WITHOUT A PLAN
> IS JUST A **WISH.**
>
> ANTOINE DE SAINT-EXUPERY

A plan. Everyone needs to have one. Most of us build our days around them. So, when it comes to our business, why is it so hard to put something formal together? There are so many terms and definitions to "planning" it's enough to make your head spin. So, where do you start?

Have you heard of SMART goals? If you have, great, but if SMART goals are new to you, you'll love how much more focused and productive you can be when using them.

WHAT IS SMART?

Specific
Measurable
Attainable
Realistic
Timely

Specific goals have concrete details that answer questions surrounding the topics of who, what, why, where, how, and when. *Measureable* goals give you a way to know if you've succeeded. *Attainable* and *realistic* goals can be tricky to nail down because you don't want the goals to be too comfortable or they won't be motivating; however, unrealistic goals can be just as demotivating. *Timely* goals give you a deadline to keep you on track.

Let's use my product, Bye Bye Monster, as an example and make a SMART plan for it.

Specific: children's educational product

Measurable: become the recognized brand in the space

Attainable: solve the problem of children's nighttime fears through imaginative play

Realistic: give children a nighttime defense

Timely: three years to goal

Planning basically closes the loop on the whole foundational discussion we started talking about at the beginning of this chapter. What do you do with all the research? Put it together in a formalized plan and then execute on that plan. Sounds simple, right? It's not. Planning takes time and it takes discipline. You also need to understand your plan can (and should) morph based upon what's happening in your business at any given time. A plan holds you accountable and can be used as a ruler to measure deliverables against; however, you must be flexible, and when opportunities present themselves that clearly align with the business's goals and objectives, you should feel free to add them.

SO **WHAT?**

So how does this heady planning stuff make you moo-lah? If you do a bit of research and analysis, you will be armed with enough information to make informed decisions around your business, your product, and/or service—and how you market and ultimately sell to your customer. Remember what I said at the beginning of this chapter? This "stuff," this chess playing, strategic research is not for the faint of heart.

The good news is that most skip it, which means you have an opportunity to do it right—the first time—so you can reduce or eliminate re-work along the way. You see, if you don't get it right the first time, you will need to fix it along the way.

Imagine you cut yourself and it's not just your finger, but a major artery. You wouldn't put a BAND-AID on it, would you? No. You'd put a tourniquet on it and get yourself to the hospital pronto because, if you didn't, you might bleed out. That's a bit morbid, I know, but it's the perfect example to use, because I see this kind of problem solving happening with so many small business owners. They skip the planning steps and go right to the fun stuff. They figure "they've got it," but they don't consider what will happen if their guess is wrong. Not only do they have to do it over, but doing it wrong the first time may have left a negative impression, which, in turn, could require damage control. So, instead of making them moo-lah, skipping the planning steps ends up costing them moo-lah. Lots and lots of moo-lah.

If you take nothing else away from the information in this book, remember this one thing: *You'll pay for it one way or another.* And, by "it" I mean "the work."

The beautiful thing is that you have a choice. You can choose to do it right the first time or you can pay exponentially more along the way in all the re-work you will need to do to correct the mistakes. Re-work is expensive. Imagine you build a website without having done this heady stuff and you miss the mark. What you've said on the website and how it looks do not resonate with your audience. What happens next? You have to do it again—after the money has already been spent. By the time it's re-done, you'll have paid double for the website, when if you would have invested the time in the research, you could have avoided this misstep.

So, take a deep breath and lean into the work. Just do it. When you come out the other side, you won't regret the effort. You've got this! Good luck!

BRAND BITS.

- Get clear on who you are and what you sell.

- Three Cs:
  Connecting dots = Clarity = Close.

- You need a solid foundation before you build your brand.

- A mission statement defines a company's reason for existing.

- A value proposition defines how your business solves your customers' problems.

- A SWOT is a benchmark comparison against the competition.

- Customer personas help you sell to your customer that which is personal and relevant.

- Competitive analysis is necessary to back up decisions with industry research.

- Unique differentiators give you a competitive advantage.

- SMART = Specific, Measurable, Attainable, Realistic, Timely

CHAPTER **THREE**

PICK A LANE.

There has always been a ton of confusion for my clients in and around whether they should brand their business under a corporate or a personal brand. Consequently, often they find themselves riding down both lanes and struggling with how to show up in any given situation. I hear "I'm a coach, so do I brand under my personal name or a business name?" My response is "It depends." But, the true answer is lengthier than my response. It's such a big decision that it takes multiple pages to help explain what you need to know in order to make the decision for yourself. In fact, it's an entire chapter's worth of an answer.

Many of my clients, when asked how they arrived at their decision to brand under a corporate brand or a personal brand, tell me it was an arbitrary decision with really no rhyme or reason behind it. They say their decision just felt right at the time and now they may or may not be questioning what they've chosen. If you elect to try to be both, you will be riding two horses with one arse. The problem is you won't necessarily be able to do either one well when the other one needs your attention. You'll need two budgets, two plans, even sometimes two teams of staff. Going that wide is expensive, both in money and in resources in general. It absolutely can be done, however. My friend and client, Deb has done it successfully which I will share with you a bit later in this chapter. She's able to have two brands because she has the budget and resources to do so. If you don't, you'll need to choose just one lane, either a personal or a corporate brand.

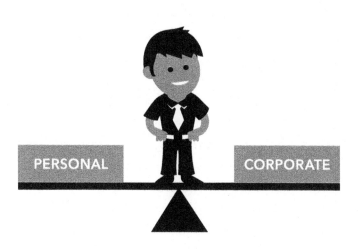

The objective of this chapter is to help you delineate what's the best choice for you. Now, having said that, your answer can be "both." Assuming it's not, I'm going to discuss each so you have a picture of both to help with your decisions. There's a movement in play that places an emphasis on personal branding, so the majority of this chapter will speak to that, but we will touch on corporate brand, as well. You might want to read through all of the information in this chapter and then go back to really glean what makes sense for your business.

There's one thing I want to make you aware of early on: it's much easier to brand a corporate brand versus a personal brand. Would you like to know why? Because it's much easier for us to talk about (and pick apart) something that isn't "personal." For various reasons, we have a hard time talking about ourselves, and that's what personal branding is entirely about: us.

Let me give you an example. Let's say I am going to give a keynote on the importance of personal brand. The very first thing I do before beginning my talk is to ask for a volunteer to come up on stage and, because I'm promising the volunteer candy, I get a lot of volunteers. When the person I've chosen gets on stage, I ask her to choose from among the three kinds of candy I have laid out for her. (I generally bring M&Ms, a Snickers bar, and Reese's Peanut Butter Cups. Inevitably, almost everyone chooses M&Ms (which seem to be the brand favorite). I ask the person to describe that candy to the audience. She proceeds to do a very enthusiastic, theatrical description of how they "melts in your mouth and not in your hand" and how they are candy coated. (Most people really know their M&Ms.) When she finishes, I ask her to describe herself. She freezes. She can barely form words. And not only is she stumped by what to say, when she does say something it's arbitrary, like the fact that she is a parent or her favorite color is blue. With a flushed face—and wishing she were anywhere else on the planet besides on my stage—she is relieved when I thank her and tell her she can have a seat. I let her off the hook.

Why do you think my volunteers can describe the candy better than themselves? In a recent talk using this example, the woman on my stage was forty-four years old—so she had had exposure to herself for four decades. You would think she'd have known herself better than anyone on the planet, yet she struggled. Why? Because we don't do well talking about ourselves. We self-sabotage or feel we aren't good enough (or worry that sharing our attributes will be misconstrued as bragging), so we audit what we say—so much so that we leave out the best parts. In the case I just mentioned, the forty-four-year-old was one of the top financial advisors in her firm of mostly men. A well-architected personal brand can be as powerful as a well-defined corporate brand, but again, only if it is done well—with "well" being the operative word—so this chapter is weighted in favor of personal branding.

PERSONAL VS. CORPORATE BRAND.

Your brand is what people say about you when you're **not** in the room.

JEFF BEZOS | FOUNDER OF AMAZON

Some business owners need a personal brand, some need a corporate brand, and some need both—but remember, I caution you on a "both" business model unless you have the infrastructure to support both brands. Even though this section emphasizes personal brand throughout, I'll start by explaining the difference between the two (personal versus corporate) and we'll touch on corporate brand in a bit.

When most people think of brand, they think of the big guys like Google or Nike, and visualize their logo, tagline, and tone of voice. How many of you think of Nike and immediately "Just do it." pops into your head? How about their swoosh? You could probably pick it out of a crowd of 1,000 logos. These identifiable markers sum up the identity these big companies want to portray to their audience. Looking at corporate brands, you might get a better picture in your mind by thinking of 3M, General Mills, or Target Corporation.

But what about personal brands? When you reduce the intentions of branding down to their most basic components, individuals can benefit from branding just as much as organizations.

Let's review some of the ways a personal brand can benefit you. As a leader, your brand becomes an important determining factor in how many followers you have. If we think about world leaders and—for illustrative purposes—use past presidents of the United States as our example, we can say that we immediately know what they stood for, what they believed in, their platforms, a bit about their personal lives, their general preferences, how they appeared in public, how they articulated their ideas, and so forth. All of those individual components wrapped up with a bow are the essence of their personal brands, and it is the parts—as well as the whole—that made the American people vote for them or against them. Each president's brand resonated stronger with a majority of US citizens (or at least more than any other candidate) which is why he was elected.

With every president's personal brand contributing in part to his election, there are also, typically, some misrepresentations. You know the ones, like the TV ads from their political rivals that run over and over (and over) depicting alleged misdeeds or attacks on character. Do those affect a candidate's personal brand? You bet. It's a constant battle to protect a president's personal brand so it constantly aligns with what they profess they will do for the people of the United States. Every move candidate's make is documented online, in the media, and in print which leaves a lifelong digital footprint.

Consider President Franklin D. Roosevelt, who was paralyzed from the waist down due to a condition thought to be the result of polio. During his presidency, he wanted to make sure the public knew he was a capable leader, considering disabilities were frowned upon in the 1920s. So, he created a system for him to appear to "walk" to the podium for speeches. FDR requested the press avoid photographing him walking, maneuvering, or being transferred from his car. "The stipulation was accepted by most reporters and photographers but periodically someone would not comply. The Secret Service was assigned to purposely interfere with anyone who tried to snap a photo of FDR in a 'disabled or weak' state.[10] He needed to protect his personal brand.

The same need for brand protection goes for you and me, only on a less grand scale. You see, everything you post about yourself online—general information, images, and the like—is permanent, and you should be consciously aware of what is "out there" about you—as well as anticipating any outcomes of what is yet to evolve. Did you know that according to a study by the computer security company AVG, 92 percent of children under the age of two already have a digital footprint?[11]

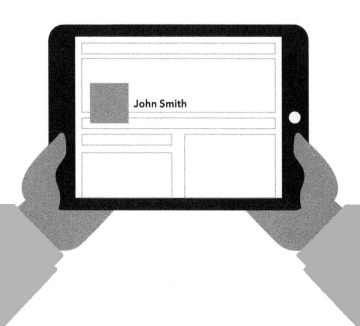

If you are looking for a promotion or a job change, your personal brand will have as much to do with the decision as your ability to do the work. There are lots of people who could match your résumé apples to apples and it's often personal brand that sets the stronger candidate apart from the pack. How does an employer decide which personal brand he or she prefers? It is the one that resonates with the business culture the best. When I was hiring and managing sales teams across the country, I would have dozens of interviewees all puffed up and proud about their shining résumés full of sales statistics and record-breaking moments during their sales careers. In each case I would tell them the exact same thing: "You wouldn't be sitting in front of me today if you couldn't sell. I only interview the best of the best in sales talent. How I will make this hiring decision is based upon how you blend with and adapt to our corporate culture. I want you to spend the next thirty minutes wowing me with what kind of person you are, how you think, what you feel, your compassion, your perseverance, your collaboration. Those are the things I'm looking for." If they would have known what I really meant, I could have easily saved myself five minutes of explanation and simply said "Tell me about your personal brand." (I suppose you're wondering what my applicants did? Well, after they picked their jaw up off the floor, they responded in similar fashion to the keynote candy example I mentioned earlier. They had a very, very difficult time, sharing relevant, personal information about themselves.)

With corporate brands, you have three goals: to gain awareness, to build trust, and to earn loyalty. Believe it or not, these are the same goals for a personal brand, but there are differences between them. The first step in making a choice between a personal brand and a corporate brand is to have a clear understanding of the similarities and differences, so let's look more closely at corporate brand.

CORPORATE BRAND.

Corporate brands are different from personal brands in that the corporate brand represents an entire entity and the individuals working at the corporation who support the overarching brand. Branding on a corporate level allows for increased awareness and consistency in the market. The deciding factor when choosing a corporate brand over a personal brand is the desire to have the corporate identity "survive" the founder. Take Oprah for example. Oprah has founded many corporate brands including Harpo Productions and OWN (the Oprah Winfrey Network). Oprah is her personal brand. Have you heard of the 'Oprah Effect'? Basically, it's an expression used to describe what often times happens to people and companies who get Oprah's attention. In many cases, they can find overnight success through her promotion of them or her endorsement. If Oprah passes away, that 'Oprah Effect' magic does, too. However, Harpo, Inc. (her parent corporate brand) and all of her sub-brands—if managed correctly—could survive.

Under a corporate brand structure, you have the flexibility of creating sub-brands. Oprah, for example, has numerous sub-brands, including:

- OWN: The Oprah Winfrey Network
- O, The Oprah Magazine
- O at Home
- Oxygen Media
- The Angel Network
- Harpo Productions, Inc.
- Oprah Winfrey Leadership Academy

I imagine the list will keep growing, since she is a powerhouse mogul.

As customers gain more access to general company information (especially via the Internet), they also develop a greater demand for details about that business's founder. That's why you need to take the time to craft your personal reputation in order to create a personal brand that is parallel to your company's brand.

PERSONAL BRAND.

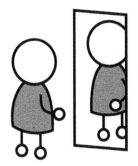

Can you answer these two questions?
1. **What are you known for?**
2. **What happens because of you?**

Try to think of personal branding like a marketing strategy focused on you. So often we concentrate on everything but us; however, when it comes to personal branding, you have to be the priority. Part of the challenge is figuring out who you really are (this includes your values, passions, personality, and skills), who you want to serve, and how you are special, unique, and different.

In Minneapolis, where I live, there are many companies and individuals that do what I do. It's a very creative town, so there are lots of options to choose from if you need creative services; however, there are a few things I feel set me apart from the pack.

I'll describe my differentiators (the things that make me different and special) on the next page. For yours, ideally you would have four.

KELLY
LUCENTE

I am a disruptor. I don't do vanilla, so if you want more of the same, you shouldn't hire me. I disrupt the status quo. Why? To get noticed. To stand out. To help my clients be perceived as influencers in their space. I'm hardwired to notice what is different, and that is one of my specialties.

I think differently. Frequently, in corporations the sales and marketing departments don't get along. They often have opposing agendas. You might not expect that, given the nature of their roles where marketing supports sales' efforts. However, it's like the chicken and the egg analogy: Which comes first? If you ask each team, they'll answer that they do; when, in fact, they need to work together to achieve the goal. I'm always looking at marketing strategy from a sales perspective because I think with both the marketing side and sales side of my brain equally. Getting the job done is about connecting the dots and using both skill sets.

I'm all in. When you hire Re-Tool Marketing, you get me. Many agencies that are my size don't have their CEO working with the clients. In other words, those CEOs are more "behind the scenes." I'm eyebrows deep in the trenches with my clients. My team supports my directive and they execute on my plan. It may seem a little like "Big Brother," but I have twenty-five plus years of experience with Fortune 500 brands and I want my clients to feel they are getting that experience in their business.

I lead with strategy. Those who know me know I'm a big fan of StrengthsFinder 2.0. As a result, I only add to my core team those who have "strategic" as one of their Top 5 themes—even the creatives. Why? Because the "strategics" find the shortest distance to the answer and that skill can't be taught. You're either born with it or not. My team was born with it.

Let's use another example. What if we were to compare superheroes, say the difference between Batman and Iron Man (my personal fave). Both are billionaire playboys, so why would we choose Iron Man over Batman if we needed superhero services?

Iron Man is an engineer. Not only does he build his own suits, but he's capable of making weapons of mass destruction.

He is a leader. He is the clear leader of the superhero team The Avengers. Other superheroes look up to him and he is the guy who establishes the plan of attack, so he's innately strategic.

Iron Man can travel at the speed of sound, which means he can get where he needs to be quickly. Batman would need to take his car.

He's sensitive. Outwardly, he doesn't show it, but Tony Stark (Iron Man's alter ego) is a sensitive guy and his internal vulnerability has him look at things through a different lens and—even though he's a bit narcissistic—he still has a big heart and he does lead with it.

How fun was that? You could practice breaking down what sets apart your own "faves" before diving into your own personal differentiators.

Personal branding oozes from your every orifice. I'm serious. It's how you communicate, how you look, what you believe, the tribes you follow, your interests, your passions and values, and your strengths, weaknesses, and preferences. Personal branding is about identifying and communicating all of that in a way that is uniquely you. But, your personal branding is also about managing the brand once it's defined. Keep in mind your personal brand is established in the minds of others from the first impression to the last impression. Authenticity is central when defining your personal brand because if it isn't naturally you, the real you will show up over time and in various ways when you aren't fully aware or are even looking. The discrepancies will confuse your audience and, thus, hinder your ability to position yourself as a niche expert.

YOU ARE A BRAND.

WHO ARE YOU?

You are a personal brand whether or not you're promoting it actively online or offline. It exists. It exists with the people who know you, with your past employers, with friends, family, and their acquaintances, too. When someone mentions you in conversation to someone else, they are expressing their understanding of your personal brand—what you do, what you're passionate about, and what you are known for.[12]

A BRAND EMBODIES MANY THINGS.

When you think about the facets of your brand, you need to look at everything about you that impacts who you are and how you "show up" in the world—whether physically or virtually. This includes many aspects:

- Image
- Style
- Reputation
- Perception
- Character
- Vocation

Have you ever spent time, serious time, analyzing everything that makes you *you*? The impact of your brand is very powerful, whether you are doing anything about managing it or not. Think about the times you've been on Facebook and seen pictures of your business colleagues looking provocative or saw them participating in a heated rant. Those moments are lasting—even though they captured a single moment in time.

WHAT DOES PERSONAL BRAND LOOK LIKE?

For celebrities, or those in the public eye, it's easy to demonstrate what personal brand looks like. Take four famous people, for example, whom we could call out and easily list what they are known for:

> **Will Smith**, aka The Fresh Prince, is the actor/songwriter who would never use a swear word in his rap music out of respect for his grandmother. He exudes positivity and open/fair mindedness.

Marilyn Monroe was the sex symbol of the last century. Need we say more?

Princess Diana was a role model for all women who wanted to break tradition and express independence and moral integrity. She championed many taboo issues that needed a voice.

Brad Pitt is actor/activist who looks good, does good, seems to be charmed in every way, and has a boatload of kids. "Family first" is his public motto, and he has spear-headed many philanthropic efforts, having created the Make It Right Foundation to re-build New Orleans.

In each case, these well-known pop culture figures probably have (or had) a team of handlers managing their brands on a daily basis. They are/were in charge of growing the brand as well as conducting damage control when things go/went bad. Think about Lindsay Lohan and what comes to mind? Is it her brilliant portrayal as bright-eyed separated sisters in the remake of *The Parent Trap*, or is it her period of treatment when she was at her lowest?

Or how about superheroes? In the illustrations, I bet you can name each superhero shown without their names being revealed. You immediately can identify the rich guy with a sidekick, the one bitten by an insect, the one frozen for seventy years, and the one with amazing strength who comes from another planet. Describing each of them by their personal brand attributes is easy as pie. Why? Because those attributes have been described, defined, lived out in print and onscreen, and discussed in daily conversation among the heroes' fans.

SHOULD YOU CHOOSE A PERSONAL BRAND?

1. Can your business be bigger than you?

If you see the business being bigger than you (and surviving you), corporate branding should be a priority. If you don't see your business scaling beyond your involvement with it, then personal branding is perfectly okay.

2. What type of business structure do you have (sole proprietorship, LLC, one-person consultant, multi-person partnership) and do you want to sell the business eventually (as part of an exit strategy)?

If you plan to stay with your business for the rest of your professional career, personal branding might be the way to go. If you eventually want to sell it, you should consider corporate branding.

3. How do you envision growing your business? Where do you see it going?

Having a solid plan in place prior to deciding on your brand is prudent in determining which to choose. Knowing the end result will help you at the front end.

4. Are clients only hiring you (or paying a premium) because of you?

If people hire your business so they can work with you and your expertise, personal branding is absolutely acceptable. But if people are hiring your business for other reasons, corporate branding is your best bet.

IS A PERSONAL BRAND RIGHT FOR YOU?

Everyone has a personality, but not everyone has a personal brand. Strategically nurturing your personal brand to maximize your potential can make you relevant, different, unique, and remembered. At the core, a personal brand is what you stand for and reflects how you choose to be perceived. One of the great things about personal branding is its authenticity. By actively cultivating your brand, you control how you are perceived by others. Personal brands showcase what you're known for, and that, in turn, increases your credibility as a professional. Defining yourself in such a distinct way allows you to become an established character that people look to as an influencer.

PERSONAL BRANDING IS NOT FOR EVERYONE.

There's another side of personal brands in small business called "vanity branding." In these cases, people want to look, feel, and sound like an expert, but what they don't realize is they've taken a "me, me, me" approach. This comes off to outsiders as self-serving and can result in the brand being overlooked or rejected by potential customers, because what customers want is a "them, them, them" approach.

What causes this is when personal branding is done too early, with no long-term plan. When you brand a personal brand too early, the brand hasn't been established long enough for you to have "proof of expert" status, meaning that during the early stages of personal branding, there are few (if any) successes to ensure proof of worth on a social scale.

Of course, personal branding isn't always necessary, and depends on the industry and the business you are in. People in some careers require it (celebrities, authors, speakers, and consultants, for example). In those cases, people are hiring them because of who they are and their experience and expertise. In other industries, such as service providers, you might find a corporate branding approach is best.

THE **POWER** **3** IMAGE + VOICE + PROMISE
OF **3** = PERSONAL BRAND

Now that you have a general understanding of what a personal brand is, let's dissect its parts. Let's take a look at how your personal brand is communicated and reflected. There are three parts to consider: brand image, brand voice, and brand promise.

BRAND IMAGE.

Brand image is what people see. It includes your style, clothing and accessories, and your smile. It's your body language, posture. This goes for everyone—both women and men. At first glance a person who's never met you before will size you up and make assumptions about you based upon your appearance and personality—whether those assumptions are true or not. Take a look at my friend, Christine.

These pictures were from a recent photo shoot I art directed for her personal brand as a ghostwriter to the stars. Notice how we incorporated props into the shoot, as well as highlighted her styling to include hair and wardrobe. I wanted to reflect through her pictures how she shows up in person. For her, it's all about the "words" and so we used letters and a feather pen writing words, but also demonstrated her fun and flirty side. Personality has to show up—whatever that looks like.

BRAND VOICE.

Brand voice can be both verbal and nonverbal. It includes communication skills and attitude. Think about all the places you use your brand voice:

- LinkedIn, Facebook, Twitter and other social networks
- Email
- Thank you(s)
- Your personal greeting
- Your email signature
- How you introduce yourself (or how others introduce you)
- Your elevator pitch
- The tone and execution of your communications
- Your vocabulary and vernacular

As I mentioned earlier, when talking about the colleague having a social rant on Facebook, his or her moment of passion is now forever etched in cyberspace. Is that a bad thing? Unless you are a shock jock, most definitely. It's one thing to react in the heat of the moment when no one is around or listening. That kind of outburst disappears as soon as your blood pressure comes down. However, if you make your feelings known publicly—especially if they aren't your feelings regularly (but only in the heat of the moment)—that momentary perception of you becomes others' reality of you because it never, ever goes away. Others will be able to refer to it whenever they want. I'll give you a recent example: my son told me about a Facebook post he had seen. It was a millennial's debate over a government ruling. One boy's rant generated responses from many other people weighing in. I asked him where I should look on Facebook to see it, and he said, "Don't worry, Mom. I screen grabbed it all. I'll pull it up in my photos."

Remember the Internet is permanent. Anything you say or do can be used against you.

BRAND PROMISE.

Your brand promise is your life and work experience combined and how you perform through your behavior is a direct reflection on your personality and ultimately others' opinions of you. Think about how your brand promise shows up in everyday life:

- Your behavior
- Your personality traits
- Your skills and the level of those skills
- How you engage with others
- Your work product
- How you follow through
- How you show up and participate at meetings
- Your energy level
- Your reputation
- Your character

Are you seeing a pattern here? The sum of the parts—image, voice, and promise—make up your personal brand. Every part of you and your participation in life is a reflection on how you are perceived.

Do your due diligence every day to influence that perception by always showing up authentically and with purpose. Your personal brand is something that needs attention 24/7. It lives and breathes without your support, but make sure you are the driver.

TO PERSONAL BRAND OR TO NOT,
THAT IS THE QUESTION.

Personal branding may not be right for you—or at least not yet. Some of the most successful brands develop their corporate brand first, with their personal brand naturally following suit. Apple, for example, was branded first. Then, came Steve Jobs. Microsoft came first, Bill Gates came second. How do you know which way to go? Well, let's look at some examples.

ALIGNING THE TWO.

I have worked with many clients who have required both a personal and a corporate brand. Let me share an example.

> Chef Deb started her business as SAVOR Culinary Services, a boutique catering and dietary consulting service focused on medically necessary and healthy diets. She has a full staff dedicated to providing food to families and servicing that side of her business. However, because of her success and unique focus in a specific niche in her industry, she is frequently asked to speak, author, and be an expert contributor as "Chef Deb,"

a personality brand. As a result, we needed to create a personal brand that reflected her as an individual brand–separate from the corporate brand–to support the high level of interest in her point of view. In other words, because she is perceived as an influencer in the medicinal culinary space, there is an expectation of hearing what she has to say. It needed to be positioned separately for maximum impact.

Her two sister brands:

The intended audience and message determine which of Deb's brands takes center stage. In the following print ad, Deb needed to be positioned as a thought leader speaking about the importance of learning about food if a person has food intolerance. Notice we lead with her personal brand, but the test lives on her corporate-branded site, so the ad is reflected as such.

Building a corporate brand goes through the same process as building a personal brand in that the strategic exercises are the same, with the caveat that there are usually corporate rules and/or compliance requirements for you to follow to fit within the corporate culture, as well as to act as a representative of the corporate brand. It's important to understand how your corporate and personal brands interrelate. If you work for a large company, you might find some elements of the two brands are in conflict. That's okay—as long as you're aware of this conflict you can take steps to manage your personal brand message the way you want.

There are easy things you can implement right now regarding your personal brand, though, so let's focus our energy there.

GET **GOOD HEADSHOTS.**

Good headshots means more than taking a selfie with your smart phone. Getting good headshots starts with interviewing photographers to review their aesthetic to ensure they can capture your brand essence. If you are going to invest in professional shots, you should consider having someone help you with hair and makeup because camera-ready makeup is very different than everyday makeup. Make sure you get a good range of shots to build a small image library. Five to six pictures using two different outfits would be ideal (three shots in each). Shoot on a solid white background, as well as a textured one, using various poses. And make sure your photographer gives you both color and black and white versions of your images.

Why do you need multiple shots? You need multiple shots so that each can be used in very specific mediums. For example, you would use a textured background image on your "about me" page of your website, but you'd use a white background for all of your thumbnail images throughout all social media.

Why is that important? Because you need to have a consistent visual representation across all mediums so people immediately know it's you. If you use a variety of pictures: a personal one of you hugging a girlfriend in Cabo on Facebook, a cropped image of the most professional one you have in your personal pictures for LinkedIn, and so on, it makes it very difficult for people to pick you out of the crowd. Remember that you are competing with a sea of the same—and it's very choppy and noisy water. If you aren't on top of this, you'll be overlooked, you won't be taken seriously, and you'll miss opportunities.

You'll also need additional pictures (preferably from the same shoot, but in a different outfit) to keep on hand to use for your speaker sheet, bio, media kit, and any miscellaneous needs you may encounter for your personal brand to be front and center.

Pricing varies from photographer to photographer, so be sure to check their fees and any add-ons. You'll also want to take a look at previous work they've done, which is similar to your project. You want to be sure you find someone seasoned in shooting professionals. Every photographer has a specific style and you need to make sure it works with yours. If it doesn't, the shots will look forced.

BEFORE

AFTER

Check out Nicole's shoot. She is a personal chef, so we needed to shoot her in her chef coat, as well as her street clothes. Her corporate brand involves her chef attire, but there is also a need for professional shots with her in street clothes because she's not in her chef coat 24/7. These images will live in a variety of places, including social media thumbnail images, bio, speaker sheet, media kit, website, and any press requests.

You have your .com, you know your strengths, you're clear on your story, you have a great image library, now what?

KNOW **YOUR TRIBE.**

I am borrowing the term "tribe" from Seth Godin, who really captured something. In his book, *Tribes*, he argues that now, for the first time, everyone has an opportunity to start a movement—to bring together a tribe of like-minded people and do amazing things. There are tribes everywhere, all of them hungry for connection, meaning and change.[13]

Do you belong to clubs, religious groups, or any networking organizations or associations? Are you an Apple user or PC? Do you drive a BMW or a VW Bug? Do you prefer Coke or Pepsi? Take another look at LinkedIn. At the bottom of your profile, you have the opportunity to become a member of groups. Once you start joining and you have yourself a healthy collection, when you look at the whole, what do you see? A person who specializes in anything specific, or a generalist?

If you become a member of a group, you are attached to their beliefs and brand direction. If they change their philosophy, you need to know that so you can make a decision to stay involved or move on. I am a member of networking organizations and found myself on the homepage of one of their websites for over a year, which was wonderful exposure. However, if they had changed or altered their agenda or messaging so it did not align with my personal and professional beliefs that could have been problematic for me, because many people knew I was associated with them—including the organization's 10,000+ person membership.

Make sure you do your homework before agreeing to attach your brand somewhere and, when possible sign agreements stating you do not agree to waive your rights on how your brand is being used. I've had numerous clients come to me with contracts after the commitment was in motion—book chapter written and promoted, speaker lineup advertised, exhibitor booth paid for—with a surprise waiver in it, and with an expectation to sign. I say, "no." No. No. No.

For example, once you agree to write a chapter in a book, which you do not control means you are at the mercy of what someone else does with that book. If it gets bad reviews, you get bad reviews. In reverse, if it's a best seller, you're a best seller. Along the same lines, if you partner at an event, the same applies. If you are not the event organizer, you are not in charge and you may even have to pay a fee to participate, whether it's in speaker fees, exhibitor fees, or through a percentage of the sales.

Now that you know how to get your personal brand where you want it to be, make sure to keep one eye on it. Be mindful of the collective impression and mutterings about you so you can ensure your brand aligns exactly how you want it to. Help others if you can when you see them going down a dangerous personal branding path and be authentically proud of who you are because you are special—so share it with the world!

SO **WHAT?**

Now that you've learned about the differences between personal and corporate branding and how the two intersect, you should understand what a strong brand looks like and where yours has been prior to reading this chapter. If you've been working as you've been reading, by now you've re-Freshed your story and updated your virtual presence. Give yourself a hand! This is hard work. Why is it harder than some of the other brand building suggestions I'm making to you? Because personal brand solely focuses on you and each of us is our hardest brand to build and the toughest subject to talk about.

So how does knowing the difference between a personal and corporate brand—and building accordingly—make you moo-lah? Again, it's about clarity. Getting really clear on your lane helps your audience be clear on what you can deliver. As I've stated before, it's very difficult to ride two horses with one arse. Not impossible, but difficult. It's difficult because unless you have two teams with two budgets and two plans, the "one" of each you have will need to be split across two initiatives. By picking a lane and staying there, all of your efforts are focused, which also reduces room for error.

There's a lot of gray in balancing both or being unclear about the one you picked. By being certain—being decisive and owning your decisions—you operate in black and white. And that's where the magic happens.

BRAND BITS.

- Corporate brands represent the entire entity.
- Corporate brands can survive their founder.
- Personal brands are made of people, not concepts.
- Personal brands showcase what you are personally known for.
- What you post online is permanent.
- You're a personal brand whether you do anything about it or not.
- Power of 3: Image + Voice + Promise = Personal Brand
- Tribes give you connection, meaning, and opportunity.
- Perception is reality.
- It's hard to ride two horses with one arse.

CHAPTER **FOUR**

YOU'RE NOT A GRAPHIC DESIGNER AND NEITHER IS YOUR COUSIN SUE.

> ## GOOD **DESIGN** IS
> ## GOOD **BUSINESS**
> **THOMAS J. WATSON JR.** | PRESIDENT, IBM

Any time I attend a networking event and tell people I build brands, there are several people who respond with, "Branding is so important. Thank goodness there isn't anything wrong with mine." And so it goes. Nobody thinks their kids are ugly—and they certainly don't want to hear that they are from someone they've just met. Sadly, sometimes I have to deliver bad news to the parents who birthed their own brands without any professional assistance. It's a difficult conversation, which often leaves the recipients with looks of shock and horror on their faces. I try to explain they did the best they could with the information they had, but if they wish to grow their business, sometimes changes need to be made. So how do you know if your business uses good design? First, you need to understand what "good design" is and how it works.

Remember the "building a house" analogy in chapter 2? Well, let's keep that conversation going a bit longer. Typically, you'd hire an architect to draw up plans before you dig a hole in the ground, right?

What happens if you do it yourself and bring in an expert midway through the process who says your basement is too shallow? I actually witnessed that when I was in the homebuilding industry. A house went up in haste and, during the final walk-through the homeowners noticed the basement ceiling was lower than the nine feet they paid for. It had been missed on the blueprint. The builder had a completed home—all the way through landscaping—and the homeowner said, "Raise it up. We want nine-foot ceilings in the basement." Well, guess what? It was too late to simply "fix" it. The only thing to do was to either live with it as it was, or tear the house down to the foundation and add several rows of block. Ultimately, the homeowners moved in with the lower ceilings, but the builder wrote a check in compensation for the error. The moral of the story is that making mistakes costs money.

In a design scenario—just like in that house—the extra cost lives in re-work. You see, design makes or breaks the user experience. They either like what they see and understand it completely—or they don't. Rarely is a reaction ever lukewarm. Investing in good design efforts up front will prevent costly re-work down the road. Without considering how design impacts the final product, service, or user experience, you might be headed for a disappointment, or worse, a disaster. I've seen bad design really negatively impact the ability to sell. The feedback I often hear is: "I didn't get it." or "I didn't think they were a serious business." How you appear is a direct reflection on how you are perceived because, in design, perception is reality.

SO YOU'RE HERE TO MAKE ME LOOK PRETTY.
-KATNISS EVERDEEN

I'M HERE TO HELP YOU MAKE AN IMPRESSION.
-CINNA

Have you ever seen the movie, *The Hunger Games*? There is a very interesting scene that ties back to good design. In the first movie, Katniss Everdeen voluntarily takes her younger sister's place in *The Hunger Games*, a televised competition in which two teenagers from each of the twelve Districts of Panem are chosen at random to fight to their death. Early in the movie, Katniss has to be presented to the people at the Capitol and she's been assigned a stylist. When she asks him if he was there to make her look pretty, he responds with, "I'm here to help you make an impression." So what was Cinna, the stylist saying? That it isn't enough to look pretty. Katniss needed to leave a calculated "feeling" with the audience so they would sponsor her giving her a better chance to stay alive longer in the game. Good design does the same thing and we'll discuss it at length in this chapter.

Unfortunately: you will pay—one way or another. You'll either pay to have your brand designed right up front or you will spend exponentially more down the road in all the re-work. Consider this: it has been my experience that every dollar invested up front in doing brand work right the first time saves four dollars on the back end. So why not spend the moo-lah on design today—unless you have the budget to spend four times as much down the road.

Design has a direct impact on why people buy, as I shared in the Katniss example. Think about it. When you look at jewelry, you immediately know whether you like it or not. Whether it's pretty or not—pretty enough for you to buy it regardless of cost. How many times have you purchased something based upon how it looked? Design is equally important in combatting the competition. If you are selling a product or service that is apples to apples in com-parison to your competition, if yours "looks" better and/or "feels" better, it will seem better than the other, which gives you a higher probability of a pur-chase. (And let's not forget that if it seems better, the consumer will instinctively expect to pay more for it. Win-win.)

In this chapter, you will learn what makes good de-sign and which parts of design are necessary to set your business apart. You will learn perception is, in fact, reality to your audience, and good design can open doors–doors that lead to conversations that can lead to sales.

THE IMPORTANCE OF
GREAT DESIGN.

ONE EYE **SEES**
THE OTHER **FEELS**

PAUL KLEE | SWISS-GERMAN PAINTER

Believe it or not, great design is a bottom-line investment. Now more than ever companies need to give serious consideration to design as it relates to how they show up and compete in the marketplace, because today's innovation is inextricably linked with design. It has become a decisive advantage in many industries and a crucial tool to being special and unique.

Apple does an amazing job at using their design to impact their audience. Their rise offers important lessons about today's connection between design and business. They have perfectly demonstrated that our desire for exceptional technology is only part of what makes a company great in the mind of consumers. They've done it so well, that if you are an Apple user, you're thought of as one of the "cool" kids.

How can great design make you more moo-lah? Your product or service is fighting for mind space, visibility,

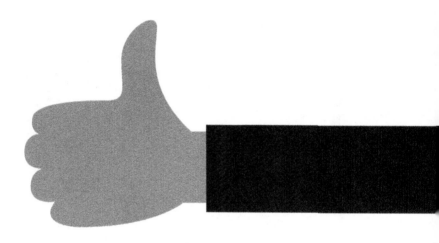

and the opportunity to prove your product or service is the one your customer must notice, try, and love. Is your brand's design getting you noticed? What kind of impression does it leave? Does it begin conversations? Does it answer questions and connect the dots for your audience? In other words: does it eliminate questions in the minds of the audience as to whether or not your product or service is the right choice for them?

Good design is one-half closing the loop for people.
(The other half is positioning and messaging.) Take a
look at the before and after example, below. The "before" doesn't give the reader any indication of where
they should go next or what they should read on the
website. It's generic and bland.

BEFORE

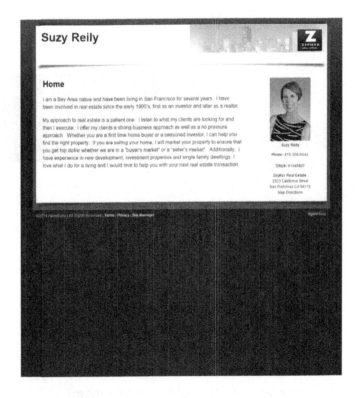

The "after" has very specific calls to action and visuals that create a level of interest in moving through the site. It demonstrates credibility, resources, and thought leadership in the space of real estate in the San Francisco area (which is the business example here). Notice the layout of information and design choice, which are very applicable for the market.

AFTER

If you want to improve your design take these three steps:

STEP ONE: HIRE A TRAINED, SEASONED GRAPHIC DESIGNER.

Whatever you do (and if you take away nothing else but this regarding design), hire a professional designer. There's a phrase I like to use: "Unless you're a graphic designer, you're not a graphic designer, and neither is your cousin, Sue." What I mean by this is that most people think they can design for themselves, or that they have a friend or family member who is really crafty and can design for them. I wouldn't consider watching an open-heart surgery on YouTube and thinking I could perform one. The same goes for those thinking they are designers, who haven't been schooled in the practice.

You see, graphic designers create visual concepts to communicate ideas that inspire, inform, or captivate consumers. They are trained not only in what to look for aesthetically, but also to get inside the consumer's head to elicit a specific brand response. They know how to set up and prep files, how to work with printers, and how each design will render based upon the medium where it is being used (for example, how your design would look on a mug versus embroidered on a garment).

They know scale, balance, and color. *They* know. We don't.

Take a look at the logo design below. The one on the left has very clean and distinctive lines. It even utilizes negative space to give the illusion of an actual knife; interesting use of space and typography. A great logo is one you'd consider wearing on a t-shirt! The one on the right does not utilize a professional or interesting typography. It's too thin and difficult to read. It was designed to resemble the cross-section of an actual butter knife, but it's hard to distinguish. If it's difficult to figure out and the dots don't connect, this confusion will cause doubt in people's minds.

GOOD	NOT SO GOOD

STEP TWO:
REMEMBER THAT LESS IS MORE.

Let's face it: we live in a world of noise and distractions trying to compete for our attention. Consider police cars. Back in the day, all they had was one single light on the roof of their car. Now, the things light up like a Christmas tree. Have you ever wondered why? It's because they are trying to get our attention in a world where people have become desensitized to noise and lights.

Obviously, you can't add another row of red lights in the business world. Noisy and over-designed marketing pieces actually create too much stimulus for people to digest in one sitting. There are too many ads, campaigns, and promos competing for our attention. Each one seems to be louder and more complex than the next, just hoping that if they add more, use brighter colors, or try to be more clever, they'll get the attention they seek. People want peace and calm and serenity because it's different than what they get every day. They don't want to work hard to figure things out when there's already too much competing for their brain power.

That's why simple, minimalist design wins. It's so unexpected, refreshing, and easy to understand that people can't help but pause and hang around for a minute. That's all you need: that one extra minute the competition doesn't get. With so much noise in the marketplace, allowing your eyes to "rest" is something consumers crave. They don't want to have to work hard to get the information they seek. They want answers to resolve their needs quickly, and with minimal effort.

If you were flipping through a magazine, which of the next two ads would get your attention? I would venture to guess it would be the one on the left. Why?? Because it's easy on your eyes. It doesn't make you work on trying to figure out what the company wants you to know. The one on the left is a winter eyewear advertisement. Clear and simple.

WINTER LOOKS **GOOD** ON YOU!

MAPLEGROVEEYE.VISION

763.416.0622

maple grove
EYE DOCTORS

WE'VE GOT YOU COVERED.

The one on the right is trying to tell you a variety of things in a very small area of real estate. They have tried to cram as much in as possible to make sure nothing was missed. That no rock went unturned. This was, in fact, the wrong approach. What are we supposed to read first? What are our eyes supposed to focus on? What do they want us to do?

You—as a company—want to create simple, clean, minimalist, fresh, and innovative designs. You—as a customer—want the same things. These are the elements that catch our attention, and a single, focused call to action converts more sales. It's to the point, direct, and keeps things easily digestible.

STEP THREE: MAINTAIN A CONSISTENT BRAND IMAGE.

How can maintaining a consistent brand image set you apart and make you moo-lah? Because it's a "no" until it's a "yes"—which means you need to connect the dots for people. How do you do that? Have as many touch points as possible that make sense and speak to the brand and it's mission. There are a few things to consider when doing this.

START AT VALET. END AT VALET.

Have you ever gone to an event and found out they had free valet parking? Even though you didn't expect it, you're able to get out of your car right in front of the entrance and some nice people make your car disappear and bring it right back to you when you need it next. How does that experience make you feel? Well, if you live in a winter climate like me, it's pretty fantastic. I stay warm AND save my shoes.

Think about your customers' experience from every point of entry. Imagine they start by learning about your brand on social media, through a friend, or from your website. What does the user experience look like for them? What does it feel like? Does it represent your brand correctly? Does it feel like a natural progression throughout the varied online properties? How about the experience at the event? Are there servers coming to you with beautiful trays of food for you to try? Is the food easy to eat while you stand holding your drink and a cell phone? Is it messy? Is there lots of garlic? Are the floors carpeted, or is it slippery to walk in your wing tipped shoes? Is there adequate seating or standing room only? How loud is the music? How many bathroom stalls are available to guests? When you want to leave how long does the valet take to get your car? These details need to be considered because they impact the whole experience.

The same planning should apply when considering your brand. Start to finish—and then start to finish again on the next engagement—each touchpoint matters. In every step, or in each case, your customer is sizing you and your brand up based upon how they "feel" about their experience.

Look at all of the touchpoints your customer will encounter along the path of experiencing your brand. Does your website sound and look like how you claim to do business? Does your collateral match the website and mirror what your brand promise is to the client? Do you and your team match the brand when they are encountered in person? Does every part of your business ooze your brand and the business mission? Remember that it starts *and ends* with the valet.

BE CONSISTENT.

| **2%** of sales are made on the **1st** contact | **3%** of sales are made on the **2nd** contact | **5%** of sales are made on the **3rd** contact | **10%** of sales are made on the **4th** contact | **80%** of sales are made on the **5th-12th** contact |

Consumers need to see components of your brand numerous times, with consistent look, tone, and feel of the brand and its various campaigns in order to earn their trust. If the appearance varies, doubt in the mind of the consumer creeps in.

Not only is consistency of great significance, but frequency as well. Have you ever heard of "The Marketing Rule of 7"? In the 1930s, Hollywood film executives realized in order to compel people to leave their homes and visit a theater to see a movie there had to be multiple touches through publicity and advertising. This idea has been passed down in the marketing world, and the number seven was adopted because it was found that around 80% of sales are made around the seventh connection.[14] Since you have to get in front of your customers at least seven times, your design needs to be consistent throughout so they know it's your business in front of them each time.

DIFFERENTIATE YOURSELF FROM THE COMPETITION.

Your brand is who you are and what you will promise to deliver, so it should have a very specific look, tone, and feel. Sometimes it can be hard for a potential customer to differentiate one brand from another in a highly competitive market—especially when products and packaging are almost identical. This is where consistent brand design can help you set yourself apart from the competition. Your colors, typography, tone of voice, and imagery should all be unique to your brand, and the messaging that defines your brand's promise should be consistent across all channels.

I have a friend who has a very successful business. In a casual conversation she commented that she was wondering why she wasn't attracting more male clients. Her products and services were heady, comprehensive, and strategic, but her entire brand identity—down to the clothes she wore—was pink. I suggested introducing some additional colors to the palette. She did, and now she has a more balanced client portfolio.

BE RECOGNIZABLE.

If you are successfully branding your business consistently, your customers will be able to recognize your brand even when it's broken apart into its components: your "brandmark" by itself (think Nike swoosh), your jingle or catchy soundbite (think McDonald's tagline, "I'm lovin' it."), or even the colors of your brand (think the Green Bay Packers' green and gold). Some people and businesses have a signature way about them that sets them apart.

If you grew up in the '70s, do you remember the term, "Dy-no-mite!" the signature saying from the television show, *Good Times*? It's been forty years and many viewers remember it like it was yesterday. And, everyone knows that the sequined glove belonged to Michael Jackson and no one else. You are crystal clear what a Hershey's kiss is shaped like, right? These are obvious examples, but examples, nonetheless, which articulate my point.

What's your recognizable "brand thing"? You should give it some thought and figure out what resonates with the business, as well as with your audience. My company, Re-Tool Marketing created this mark to live separate from the logo. Now, when anyone sees it by itself, people instinctively know it's connected to Re-Tool Marketing.

NO, MADAM.
IT TOOK ME MY WHOLE LIFE.

There is a legend that tells the story of Picasso sketching in a park when a woman approaches who recognizes him and begs for a portrait. He agrees and, a few minutes later, hands her the sketch. It has one swift and glorious stroke on the paper. She is elated at how perfectly he captured her true essence. She exclaims how beautiful it is and asks him how much she owes. He replies, "4,604 euros" (which is $5,000 in US dollars). The woman is outraged and asks how that is even possible given that it only took him five minutes. Picasso looks up, and without missing a beat replies, *"No, Madam. It took me my whole life."*

I am often asked why the design process takes so long. Well, most designers are not Picasso. They don't have a lifetime of experience which allows them to look at a piece of paper and place magic on the canvas in one stroke of the brush. It takes seasoned professionals time to think, plan, and process good design. So, let's say you get a designer: How do you ensure he or she is designing "good" design? When I instruct my design team, we consider three very specific things and you should, too—especially if you are going to attempt to design in-house or outsource to a freelance designer.

There are three steps to share with your creative team.

STEP ONE: MAKE IT RELEVANT.

Your graphic design must be appropriate for the audience it identifies. It must be relevant to your industry and the audience to which you are catering. Getting up to speed on all these aspects requires a lot of in-depth research, but the investment of time is worth it. Without a strong knowledge of your industry, you can't hope to create design that successfully differentiates you from your closest competitors.

STEP TWO: DON'T SKIP STEPS.

Don't compromise quality for deadlines by skipping over the important pieces of the process. You might want to read that sentence again. I can't tell you how many times clients have rushed a project because of an unrealistic deadline. The results were lackluster and conversion was low, if any conversions took place at all.

Designing for one piece versus an entire brand or campaign is a very different process. The designer should be involved in the process from start to finish to ensure relevancy is met (matters to your audience) and outcome is achieved (your goal and/or objective in producing the design piece). Since designers have specific aesthetics, it will be important to use the same creative team for as long as you can or ensure you have a strong brand style guide to provide to other designers so they have a roadmap and design criteria to follow to ensure they don't go off brand.

STEP THREE: CONSIDER THE OUTCOME.

Make sure you give thought to the point of the marketing piece you are designing. Try not to design for the sake of designing and push out content simply because you think you should. Many of my clients feel they need specific pieces in order to be successful such as a newsletter, sales collateral, extensive social media presence, and the like. This is only partially true. You need to fish where there are fish, right? If your audience requires newsletters, then produce a newsletter campaign. If they are on Facebook, put together a Facebook campaign. If you are a speaker and they allow you to sell in the back of the room, you need leave-behind and sales material.

HOW TO GET STARTED –
THE CREATIVE BRIEF.

When you think "creative brief" you probably think "ad agency." That would be a good association because creative briefs are a staple of most agencies. A good creative brief, however, is a vital document that should be done for every design project regardless of who's involved. Even if it's an internal project. Even if it only involves a freelancer.

Here are three reasons why you need a creative brief for every marketing project:

STEP ONE: TO SET EXPECTATIONS.

Designers can't read your mind. You need to share everything you can about your creative needs to ensure nothing is missed during the process.

A good creative brief sets expectations for the project. It answers key questions such as:

1. What is the project?
2. Why are we doing the project?
3. What are we hoping to accomplish with the project?
4. What are the deadlines for the project?
5. What action do we hope the prospect will take after seeing it?

These are questions to answer *before* the project begins so the people on the design team can understand how this project fits into the big picture of your brand. Providing a creative brief also gives your internal or external contacts the opportunity to communicate with you about deadlines and priorities so you both know what's possible.

You have to tell your design team what they need to know and set them up for success. In short, you have to set their expectations for what you are doing, how it will be done, and how much effort it will take to do it. A creative brief will help you do exactly that.

REASON TWO:
TO DEFINE YOUR AUDIENCE.

I recently had a client ask me to design two direct mail pieces to "test" the market, but they hadn't done any brand work (it was a start-up) and they weren't clear on their message or audience. Reluctantly, I agreed to do it and, when the pieces were designed, the client said, "I don't get it." If we had spent time putting together a creative brief, some of those questions would have been answered and the campaign would have been more effective.

Why wasn't the piece more effective? Because it wasn't geared to a specific audience. A marketing piece, whether or not it's a brochure, will perform better if it is focused with a specific audience in mind. A good creative brief defines the audience for the project.

The brief should have a mini description of the ideal people you are targeting, what their interests are as they pertain to your product or service, and what their pain points are. The audience description should be robust enough to put a clear picture of the prospect in everyone's mind. Then the designer can go out and create a project that's most appropriate for the audience you want to reach.

REASON THREE:
TO VISUALIZE THE DESIRED RESULTS.

Ask yourself, "Why are we doing this?" If a definitive answer doesn't materialize, you shouldn't proceed with the project. Why? Because you need to establish if your effort is to gain brand awareness or sales conversion, first, and then design around the message to support the mission. You need to be clear on the difference so you can build accordingly; otherwise, it will be confusing–to your designers and your audience.

A good creative brief is far more than a checklist or a "cut and paste" document. It sets the tone for your team and your brand. Ideally, it should start the brainstorming process and get the creative juices flowing, and it should help ensure everyone is working toward the same goal.

ELEMENTS OF YOUR
BRAND IDENTITY.

Many businesses make the mistake of believing that designing a logo is branding but branding involves so much more than that. Remember, a brand is a promise. It's a unique combination of a logo, words, typeface, color(s), personality, price, customer service, aesthetics, attitude, and voice all working together to convey the essence of what your company, product, or service stands for. A strong brand delivers a clear, credible, and memorable message. It connects with its intended audience at an emotional level. It motivates buyers and reinforces their loyalty—and your brand identity is the thing that should begin the entire design process.

TIFFANY & CO.

While the culmination of white and robin's egg blue, elegant typography, and beautiful photography create a tasteful and sophisticated look for Tiffany & Co., this same look is likely not appropriate for a footwear brand aimed at an athletic market such as Nike. It's hard to imagine Coca-Cola or Disney without their signature shapes or colors, but what else comes to your mind? Their slogans? Can you hear their jingles? The sum of the parts is what makes up brand identity.

LOGO.

A logo is quite possibly the most important strategic marketing asset a company can have. In addition to the obvious benefit of creating brand recognition, a well-designed logo can also communicate non-tangible benefits about a company. Logos can inspire people; they can instill trust and admiration, or express product or service superiority.

What some business owners don't realize, however, is that a logo should not just express what a company does but it should represent who a company "is." In this sense, a logo should be used as an asset just like any product or service provided to the public.

Corporate logos are intended to be the face of a company. They are visual displays of a company's unique identity, and through colors and fonts and images they provide essential information about a company that allows customers to identify with that company's core brand. Logos are a shorthand way of referring to the company in advertising and marketing materials; they provide an anchor point for the various fonts, colors, and design choices that are made in all other business marketing materials.

Good logos should be unique, yet comprehensible to potential customers. Although there are myriad choices for color, visual elements, and typography, in general a logo should help convey some information about the company, or be designed in a way that gives some sense of meaning about the company or its industry. For example, cutting-edge firms and technology companies tend to have angular logos to convey speed, while service-oriented firms have rounded logos to provide a sense of service and trust.

Logos are the chief visual component of a company's overall brand identity. The logo appears on stationery, websites, business cards, and advertising. For that reason, a well-designed logo can contribute to business success, while a substandard logo can imply amateurishness and turn off potential customers. However, a logo should work well with other aspects of a company's visual presentation. No logo, however well designed, can look good when surrounded by contradictory graphical elements or inconsistent fonts. This is why a logo needs to be seen as the basic unit of a larger brand identity that includes company fonts, colors, and document-design guidelines. There are three basic types of logos: a brandmark, a wordmark, and a combination mark.

"Brandmarks" (also known as icons) are simple images that are symbolic of a company. They are memorable, instantly recognizable, and illustrative. They are typically for companies that are well established and internationally known. Icons may be recognized regardless of the language spoken, and are therefore best for worldwide companies.

maple grove
EYE DOCTORS

"Wordmarks" consist of the company's name as the "logo" in a distinct font style. They are directly tied to the company and unique in design. Wordmarks are good for smaller businesses that have unique, memorable, and distinct names, and who also want to increase brand awareness. They tend to add sophistication to the brand.

US **ultimate**
SETTLEMENTS

"Combination Marks" are exactly what they sound like: a combination of both wordmarks and icons. They include a visual icon along with the company's name. Combination marks are great for companies that want a visual element to reinforce their brand, so the name and the symbol are seen together.

How can you decide which type of logo is right for you?

- **Keep it simple.** The simplest design is often the most effective. Why? Because a simple logo helps meet most of the other requirements of iconic design.

- **Make it relevant.** Your logo or other design marks such as avatars, favicons, and emojis must be appropriate for the business it identifies. What is an avatar, favicon, or emoji? A "favicon"—or browser icon—is a small image that displays next to the page title in a browser tab. Adding a favicon to your site makes your site recognizable in a browser full of tabs, and can also used by some browsers for bookmarks. An "avatar" is an image that follows you from site to site, appearing beside your name when you do things like comment or post on a blog. Avatars help identify your posts on blogs and web forums. An "emoji" is a small digital image or icon used to express an idea or an emotion in electronic communication. (Think "smiley face.")

- **Make it timeless.** Trends come and go like the wind. With your visual identity, the last thing you want is to invest a significant amount of your moo-lah in design directions that look dated within a year or two.

- **Aim for distinction.** Begin by focusing on designs that are recognizable—so much so that just its shape or outline gives it away.

- **Think small. Think big.** What will your logo look like at five inches, five feet, or fifty feet away? How about if you shrink or increase it's size? Your logo should ideally work at a minimum of one inch in size without loss of detail so that it can be put to use for many different applications. Conversely, you should consider whether it becomes pixilated when it gets bigger. (In other words, does the image become more blurry and distorted the bigger it gets?)

- **Focus on one thing.** Incorporate just one feature to help your design stand out. That's it. Just one. Not two, not three, not four. Take a look at the mark I created for my friend and client, Leo, and his company Formulaica. He is a retired F/A-18 fighter pilot, and we wanted a unique mark that

FORMULAICA™

represented where he came from and where he was headed. The brandmark uses the first and last letter of the business name, and it's designed in such a way that vaguely represents a fighter jet (past) and an arrow pointing northeast (future).

COLOR.

COLOR CREATES **EMOTION,** TRIGGERS **MEMORY,** AND GIVES **SENSATION.**

GAEL TOWEY | CREATIVE DIRECTOR, MARTHA STEWART LIVING

In marketing and branding, colors are perceived in such distinct ways that there is a whole color psychology theory surrounding it. The feelings and emotions that are triggered and translated from a color are based on personal experiences, societal norms, and culture. Effective design and use of colors can influence consumers buying habits. So naturally, when selecting color palettes, it's important to understand what emotions are translated through each color.

Because color is used to evoke emotion and express personality, it stimulates brand association and accelerates differentiation. Primary color palettes for your brand should consist of three to five colors that are utilized in your company's logo and marketing materials. These colors must be complementary to one another and selected strategically based on your company's industry and your brand's values. Secondary color palettes exist solely to complement the primary palette on marketing materials and visuals.

Brands should choose colors based on where and for what the color is being used and how they want consumers to feel when buying their products. I recently read an article at Fast Company and they were talking about the science behind color in marketing. They said," "After all, sight is the most developed sense in humans. It's only natural that 90% of an assessment for trying out a product is made by color alone."[15] (We'll address color more in a bit.)

TYPOGRAPHY.

TYPOGRAPHY

I'm silently judging your **font choice.**

Simply put, typography is the style and appearance of text. When a company is designing a brand identity, a consistent set of fonts must be used—each with a specific purpose. Fonts should be legible. They are needed for headings, titles, subtitles, and body text in any collateral—and online. Consider the weight and size of each font, in addition to the style. Serif fonts (the ones with the little tails) are easy to read and are considered more formal. Sans serif fonts (the ones that are "cleaner," without anything hanging off the ends of the letters) are more modern and come in a variety of thicknesses, styles, and lengths.

When choosing your fonts, you have to decide whether, when put together, the different fonts are harmonious with one another. Make sure they are different from your competitors and translate the personality of your brand. And, most importantly, they have to be easy to read—nobody likes invitations (to events, or to a new company) that require squinting to read.

- Header fonts should stand out the most, as they are the most important. Often, people boldface, capitalize, underline, or increase the font size to make headings pop.

- Titles should be the next text a reader sees. This font should complement the heading, but not overpower it. Consider using a slightly thinner font that is a pinch smaller in size.

- Subtitles are next. Follow a similar hierarchy when choosing different levels of subtitles as you did with the first two points, and think about italicizing the font or making it smaller in size than primary headers and titles.

- Body text is the last thing to stand out. It is crucial that body fonts are easy to read and one of the smallest in size.

IMAGERY.

Businesses need a series of images that can be used to support copy within marketing materials, on the web, and in other outbound (and internal) items. Hiring a photographer and models to do a photoshoot can be expensive, but it is often the only way to get a set of unified photographs that display your vision exactly how you wish to see it. If this is simply not in the budget, you can purchase high-resolution stock images online, but be sure to choose your images carefully and try to only select those that align in style with one another.

HOW TO CHOOSE IMAGERY.

When sourcing imagery, you need to look for a variety of things. Color, lighting, background, and the image itself should each play a huge part in the picking. One of my favorite places to source imagery is shutterstock.com. You can purchase "packages" that are quite affordable.

So, how do we put all of these creative pieces together in one location so it's easy to reference? A brand style guide.

WHAT IS A **BRAND STYLE GUIDE?**

A brand style guide is a document that establishes distinct guidelines on how all aspects of a company's brand should look, sound, and feel. It should include rules for a unified and identifiable presence for the company's brand, and should be used to help employees properly communicate the message of the brand to internal departments, external vendor partners, and the public. It should answer questions often asked by those responsible for generating forms of communication or design.

The brand style guide dictates the voice and personality of a company and governs all communication driven by the company, which can include collateral, web-driven communication, social media, advertising, design, and personal communication. This document can range from a few pages to several hundred, and should be viewed as the document that controls what the public sees from the company.

WHAT MAKES A BRAND STYLE GUIDE EFFECTIVE?

Every brand from the solopreneur to the corporate giant needs a set of branding guidelines and rules to maintain an established identity. Why? Because you don't want to leave writers and designers without direction when bringing to life materials that represent your business and your brand's aesthetic. Most "creatives" have a specific personal aesthetic and will default to those aesthetics given the opportunity. To avoid this, you want to make sure they have set guidelines to follow while allowing them to infuse work with their own creative genius.

Your brand style guide will become the "rule book" of your brand. It should be available to anyone influencing the direction of the brand and business to be used as the guideline to follow for all things visual and verbal. So, why is it necessary?

SAVES YOU TIME.

Think about it. How many times have you done something, took great notes, and found yourself referring back to them when something related came up? Imagine if you had to start over every time you encountered something that showed up more than once. Now remember your brand is something that comes up all the time. It will be tweaked, enhanced, and morphed over time to meet audience demand. You will need to create collateral and marketing efforts to continue to grow your business. Your brand style guide is the reference tool that will save you time so you don't have to start from scratch each and every time something new is created related to your brand.

HELPS YOU SHAPE YOUR CUSTOMER'S PERCEPTION.

Remember earlier in this chapter we spoke of the Marketing Rule of 7? It applies here, as it pertains to your aesthetic. Consistency is essential in forming your audience's perception of you and your organization. I'm sure you've been inside a Target store—probably more than one—and in each store, their logo is sprinkled throughout in a variety of ways with similar signage representing the latest campaign as well as relative consistency in store layout. You know where the greeting cards are, you know where the toys are, you know where to shop for groceries. This consistency is appreciated (and expected) by consumers. Target has a brand style guide and store layout guidelines among other specifications to ensure this consistency.

SERVES AS A DECISION MAKING TOOL.

When you have an opportunity to do something new, having your brand style guide to direct you will make it easier for you to make decisions. For example, if you decide to host an event and you want that event branded, you will be able to look at the brand style guide to refer to your primary and secondary color palettes to determine the parameters for choosing colors for the event.

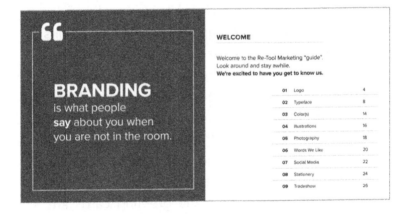

THE GUIDE(LINES).

This section will give you the framework to create your own organization specific brand style guide if you don't have a graphic designer to assist you. A company brand style guide can help ensure consistency across all documents by including specific guidelines for the following:

- Brand usage
- Writing style
- Grammar and tone
- Formatting
- Graphics

When creating your brand style guide, you should consider what is most important to your organization, corporate identity, and branding.

WHO USES YOUR BRAND STYLE GUIDE?

Anyone creating marketing material for your company should know your brand well enough to create a consistent look and feel. Whether your internal team or an outside vendor partner created your materials, a customer should be able to identify that each piece produced came from the same organization.

WHAT SHOULD BE INCLUDED IN A BRAND STYLE GUIDE?

There are some core sections to a brand style guide that should be included in yours. Let's review them.

GRAPHICS AND IMAGES

Your brand style guide should describe the overall graphics style for your designers, and give information about where they can obtain approved images. You should include photo and illustration guidelines, including acceptable file sizes and formats.

COLOR(S)

Audiences can sometimes identify a company by its combination of colors. Give writers and designers your corporate color palette with primary and secondary colors and describe which colors should be used for what. Include formats for both print (CMYK and Pantones) and web (RGB).

Of course, you will want to understand the terminology for both so you can ensure you get the right files. "CMYK" refers to the four inks used in most color printing: cyan, magenta, yellow, and key (black). "Pantone" is a brand authority on color. There are 1,755 solid (spot) colors for printing ink on paper, and there are color swatches already numbered to refer to when choosing from them. Since computers cannot "mix" colors, they need to layer the three primary colors of red, green, and blue ("RGB") on top of each other in a variety of ways on your display screen. Because of this, you will need to find an RGB number that will come close to the CMYK or Pantone colors. (It won't be an exact match, but you can get close.)

FONT(S)

Whether you have a corporate font that is unique to your company or not, you need to be able to tell designers and writers what fonts they can and should use for each document element. Body text and headings should be clearly identified with typeface, point size, and font weight.

LOGO

When looking at the logo, there are several components to consider, so we will break them down here:

Fonts & Typography

Your graphic designer and copywriter need to know how your logo will be used. You'll want to include the following guidelines:

- Maximum and minimum size (what's appropriate based upon how it looks at any particular size).
- Color or black/white usage (when it makes the most sense).
- Placement (required distance from other items).

Trademark(s)

If your company has trademarks or patents, you want to make sure you protect them by the using trademark (™) and registered (®) symbols properly. Tell writers all your trademarked and patented terms and how to use them; for example, should they include the trademark or registered symbol every time they use a specific term, or just on the first occurrence?

Writing Style

Writing style can also build your brand. While writing isn't as visual as your colors or logo, a reader should still get a consistent "feel" from all of your documents' content. What are the specifics that speak to writing style? Voice and tone, audience, and diction.

- **Voice and Tone**
  What attributes do you want your readers to think of as they read your content? That you are innovative? Cheeky? Approachable? Steadfast? Dynamic? Once you identify these attributes, tell your writers and designers so they can keep them in mind.
  Similarly, you should describe the tone of your content. Do you want it to come off professional, academic, optimistic, concise, witty, clever, or straightforward? Should writers embrace or avoid jargon?

- **Audience**
  Remind writers and designers to always consider the audience. If your audience is the same for all forms of content, include the audience's attributes and describe them in your brand style guide.

- **Diction**

The words you choose (diction) determine whether your writing is informal or formal, interesting or dry, precise or ambiguous. Describe your style preferences to your writers. You might include preferences for some of the following:

- Active or passive voice
- Articles (a, an, the) for tabs, buttons, or pages
- Conciseness
- Gender neutrality
- Point of view (first, second, or third person)

Style and Grammar Guidelines

Grammar and style are just as important as the tone of your corporate writing, so make sure that all writers are following the same set of guidelines. Many widely accepted style and grammar guidelines are available online, so no company needs to create one from scratch. Choose a style guide that best meets your needs, and instruct writers to reference this guide if they can't find an answer in your brand style guide.

Other Usage Rules

Another consideration that many first-time branders forget to consider is consistency in usage rules. Consider the following:

- **Abbreviations:** Which ones can be used, if any? What type of punctuation is required?

- **Acronyms:** What should be used? Do you spell them out on the first occurrence of the document or section?

- **Bullet points:** Should the text always start with a capital letter? How should they be spaced? Should they be introduced with a full sentence and a colon? Are you using a specific symbol to represent your "bullet"?

- **Capitalization:** What should be capitalized? Should you capitalize headings, prepositions in headings, job titles, company names, chapters, sections, plans, figures, and reports?

- **Numbers:** When should they be spelled out?

- **Punctuation:** What rules will you follow for colons, commas, ellipses, en-dashes, em-dashes, exclamation points, hyphens, quotation marks, and semicolons?

- **Serial comma:** Should there be a comma before "and" or "or" before the final item in a list?

- **Trademarks:** How will you handle the trademark and registered symbols for the products and services of other companies?

CONTENT FORMATTING.

Regardless of the size of your business, you should have templates that define your fonts, styles, colors, and formatting. This information is useful in a style guide in case someone uses a different template or would like to understand the reasoning behind your choices. Some things to consider are:

- **Bulleted and numbered lists:** How far should they be indented? What is the line spacing for lists?

- **Captions:** What format should captions follow? What items should be labeled as figures or charts?

- **Consistent organization:** Should each type of document contain specific parts such as the "So What?" at the end of each **MOO-LAH-GY** chapter?

- **Page layout:** What page layouts can or should be used? (Provide details. This is a good place for screen captures of sample layouts.)

- **Spacing:** How much spacing should be between paragraphs? How much spacing should there be in tables? (Remind writers to include one space between sentences.)

- **Styles:** What fonts, sizes, and colors should be used for each element of your document(s)? List the particular style names (H1, H2, H3, Copy) used in your document(s) such as Microsoft Word or PowerPoint. Note the style name and the characteristics of the style.

- **Tables:** What color should tables be, and what style should they follow?

SO **WHAT?**

And there you have it. Everything you ever needed to know about the importance of design and how you can create great design for your own brand.

So where's the moo-lah in good design? The marketplace is saturated with companies just like yours. So much so that there are very few who can uniquely stand out from the crowd. A question to ask yourself is: "How can a company like Coca-Cola successfully surpass all other companies to become the number one recognized and most valuable brand in the world year over year and continues to hold a position in the top five on the Forbes list?" In my opinion, one of the reasons is good design. Their logo has barely changed while their competitor Pepsi has modified their logo several times over the years.

How does design make this happen? Design creates an emotional bond between your brand and an audience with the goal of engaging in conversation—and conversation is the next step in the sales process. You see, great design helps you sell and—if you're in business—you're in the "sales" business. Cutting corners with graphic design can hurt your business. Design that has not been well thought

out and hasn't had professional input is often confusing, leaving the audience with questions which
leads to hesitation—which can be the difference between a "no" and a "yes." Good design helps bridge
that gap by connecting the dots for your audience
so that your intent is clear and meaningful.

WHEN **7** OF **10** AMERICANS RECALLED THE LAST
TIME THEY SAW A PRODUCT THEY JUST HAD TO HAVE,
IT WAS BECAUSE OF **DESIGN.**

KELTON RESEARCH

Good design helps build trust, which is the basis
for building a strong and recognizable brand. If
what you say doesn't match your visuals, there is
a disconnect in the mind of your audience. For a
solid "yes," your design has to support your business promise.

BRAND BITS.

- Good design helps build trust.
- Good design is one-half closing the loop and one-half positioning.
- Less is more.
- The Marketing Rule of 7 means seven impressions are necessary to get noticed.
- A good creative brief is necessary for design accuracy.
- Your logo is the most important strategic marketing asset you have.
- Color creates emotion.
- Images support copy. Not the other way around.
- Your brand style guide is your brand's design bible.
- Design has a direct impact on why people buy.

CHAPTER **FIVE**

IT'S A "NO" UNTIL IT'S A "YES."

 Just because you've built a brand doesn't mean you're done and everyone will want to buy. It isn't like the famous line in the movie, *Field of Dreams*: "If you build it, he will come." I wish it were that simple. No one said starting a business would be easy. It requires a great idea, innovation, marketing savvy, a competitive edge, a ton of stamina, a bit of a thick skin, and—ultimately—your business needs to provide a solution to the audience you are trying to serve.

When my son Joey was in second grade, I was eyebrows deep into my corporate career. One day I came home from work and he was crying. When I asked him what was wrong, he told me we had missed something very important at school. I asked him, "Why didn't you tell me?" And he replied, "Because you're never here." The next day, I quit my corporate job. You see, I had raised that boy alone from the time he was six weeks old and, in that moment, I realized I couldn't get the time back and so I needed to make a change—a big change that included being there for him so there wouldn't be anymore "missed moments" I couldn't get back.

It was during this time that I created Bye Bye Monster. But just because I thought it was a good idea didn't mean it was a viable business. I needed more than a cool product. I lacked the infrastructure and the financial resources to make it really go. Even though within a month from launch I found myself in Neiman Marcus's online bookstore featured next to *Fancy Nancy* and *Where the Wild Things Are*, it wasn't enough. You'd think with a win like that, a bit of press, and the added attention of Jenny McCarthy, I could make it go. Nope. So I had to say, "bye-bye" to Bye Bye Monster for a variety of reasons. First, I had a financial threshold I was not willing to go beyond—I was not willing to leverage my house or my son's college education. Second, I found myself working harder on that business than I had done in my corporate career and I had made a commitment to my son and needed to honor it. And, third, I knew it was going to take more than savvy marketing to make my business go. I needed a strong infrastructure of trusted advisors—specifically in the roles of COO and CFO—and I couldn't afford them. It was a bittersweet day when I donated my remaining inventory to charity a few holidays ago to give over six hundred children a Christmas gift.

IS YOUR'S A **WINNER?**

How many of you have tuned in to an episode of *Shark Tank*? Week after week people stand before the sharks believing they have the next big idea. Do you find yourself saying out loud, "'Why didn't I think of that?' or 'What the heck were they thinking?'" Regardless, some companies get a deal and others are sent home to continue to fend for themselves.[16]

Unfortunately, you can have the most amazing product or service in the world and fail. Why is that? How is it possible to have the next best idea to sliced bread and not "make" it? Successful businesses take more than a motivated entrepreneur and an amazing idea. It takes strategy. Now, don't get me wrong. The Pet Rock was a huge hit back in its day, selling 1.5 million pet rocks in a matter of months, but even though the inventor trademarked the name, a whole plethora of business issues derailed it as quickly as it succeeded. Could this failure have been prevented? Maybe not, but the success may have been sustained a bit longer had there been a strategy in place to address the challenges the company faced.

I recently read in Forbes that according to Bloomberg, 8 out of 10 entrepreneurs who start a business fail within the first 18 months.[17] That's not a pretty statistic—or necessarily one we want to be reminded of—but I'd rather know the odds and face them head on, so at least it won't come as a surprise if down the road I close up shop. If I've done everything right and it's still a fail, I'll sleep a little better at night knowing I did what I could with the resources I had at the time.

What can we do to circumvent the statistic? Get focused on the yes. So how do we move toward a yes?

CONNECTING THE **DOTS.**

You've heard me refer to the term "connecting dots" throughout this entire book. Honestly, it's one of the most important things you can do to get that "yes" which equates to a sale. So what does it mean? When you were young and you went to a restaurant with your family, did you get a place-mat with games on it to keep you occupied until your food arrived? One of my favorite games on the page was Connect the Dots. Remember how the picture wasn't clear until you connected all of the dots and then it finally made sense? But, you had to follow a sequence—and if you didn't fol-low it in the exact order it was numbered the pic-ture wouldn't be right. Well, the exact same thing is true in your business. Your audience views you and your product or service just like the restaurant placemat's game. They encounter you, and initially the picture isn't clear. Through exposure (some-times immediately and sometimes over a period of time), the dots begin to connect and the picture becomes clear. How quickly the picture shows up, is up to you. You have 100% control as to whether or not there is a complete picture and how soon the audience "gets" it.

This clarity comes in a variety of ways and that's what this chapter is all about. You need to touch your audience through a deep and rich dialogue, your differentiators need to be unique, and your value proposition needs to be crystal clear. You need to determine whether you provide a product or service that will resolve the customer's need, and whether you are being authentic in your delivery—throughout every touchpoint.

DEFINING THE **BIG IDEA.**

If you intend to set your brand apart, you need a big idea. "I am a coach," is not a big idea, because thousands of people claim the same thing.

In *Designing Brand Identity*, Alina Wheeler defines a big idea like this. "A big idea functions as an organizational totem pole around which strategy, behavior, actions, and communications are aligned. These simply worded statements are used internally as a beacon of a distinctive culture and externally as a competitive advantage that helps customers make choices."[18]

Don't you just love that? I sure do. Alina is basically telling us that big ideas have specific, defining characteristics. Let's take a peek at some of them.

BASED IN CUSTOMER INSIGHTS.

Your big idea must matter to your ideal customer. Whether your target is moms with small children, fellow entrepreneurs, or widowed women over 65, your big idea must be important to them in a significant way.

FIGHTS AN EVIL.

The battle between good and evil is universally compelling. Your brand must be the "good" in the fight against "evil." Women battle with their self-image on the scale (evil) and Special K gives them non-scale victories (good). Technology is complicated and frustrating (evil) but IBM makes technology accessible to everyone (good).

TURNS CONVENTION ON ITS' HEAD.

A really big idea challenges the way we think, feel, and behave. Nintendo's Wii set out to involve everyone in playing video games: grandparents next to grandkids. The idea disrupted the gaming world and created a profitable niche for Nintendo.

PUSHES THE BRAND.

If your idea fits neatly into your business's comfort zone; think bigger. Big ideas will challenge the way you deliver, communicate, and interact with your own brand. Even though Apple is currently the most-recognized brand in the world having a brand value of $145 billion second to IBM with only a brand value of $69 billion, Apple must constantly push their talent to create technology with advanced capabilities while continuing to make their products easy for customers to use and still looking good. Why? They want to hold onto their market share and know it's a competitive playing field. That's big.[19]

IS SIMPLE.

Big ideas must be expressed in words or phrases not to exceed a sentence. To distill an idea down to its essence is deceptively difficult and requires great control on the part of the brand team. The folks behind the Life is Good brand put their big idea in it's name "Life is Good." The brand simplified its mission, which is to spread the power of optimism. They believe that what you focus on will grow and they wish to grow optimism.[20] Big idea—three little words.

CREATES BUZZ.

A big idea must create buzz like the Wendy's 1984 ad campaign slogan, "Where's the beef?" That campaign was Wendy's "grand slam, home-run, bottom-of-the-ninth-in-the-World-Series" attack against McDonald's. And it worked. Wendy's pulled in a record $76.2 million in sales in 1985.[21]

To evaluate your big idea, ask yourself the following questions:

1. Have you considered all the pros and cons of your idea?

2. Have you pinpointed the specific problem your idea is expected to solve?

3. Have you tested your assumptions of the need for your idea with your target customer?

4. Is your idea fresh, original, and compelling to your target?

5. How does your idea compare to what your competitors and alternative offerings to your company offer?

6. Is your idea timeless?

7. Can you express your idea simply?

When you are satisfied with your answers to the questions above, you can congratulate yourself because you've done your due diligence on the core of what will set your business apart.

NAMING YOUR BRAND.

I work with many businesses in their startup stages. Naming becomes a big deal when the "name" is brought to life arbitrarily. In other words, when there hasn't been a formal naming session to come up with the perfect name. The naming process can be daunting, especially since most business owners want to marry their names to a .com—and so many of them are taken. You also need to determine whether your chosen name has been trademarked by another company or if you are free to do it yourself. Without that protection, you run the risk of losing your precious asset down the road.

Before you finalize your name, consider testing it with an informal group of your potential customers and ask them the following questions:

1. What do you think of when you hear the name?
2. What would you expect from a company with this name?
3. How does the name make you feel?
4. What does this company do?
5. How can this company help you?
6. Would you do business with this company?

The answers to these questions will serve as a real-world "gut check" for naming your business, which can otherwise be a very personal endeavor.

OWNING AND EXECUTING
YOUR STRATEGY.

You have an opportunity to be a brand authority in your space by being the voice of your product or service and speaking authoritatively in a variety of ways—so do it. Let's start looking at how you become a brand authority by looking at how you show up.

Remember, in chapter 2, when I asked if you were in or if you were optional? For those of you who are "in," have you hung your shingle? In other words, have you let people know you are in business? How have you done so? Are you talking about your business and the product or service you offer? How have you revealed your brand to the world? The first thing you need to do is update all of your social media platforms to utilize your new brand and create consistency. You'll want to update your website and all of your marketing materials as well so they work as a cohesive set. Make a special announcement and name it "The Big Reveal." Give it a story. Engage with others in conversation around topics specific to your areas of service. Continue to push out content that is highly stylized and on brand and, soon enough, your brand will be recognized by many! If you haven't said you are "in", how has that impacted your ability to achieve your business goals?

INTEGRATING YOUR
COMMUNICATION STRATEGY.

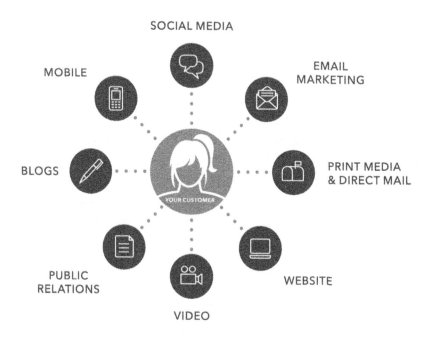

Communication. It's one of those things we all take for granted. The ability to communicate is so easy and so immediate that we don't even give it a second thought. How many of you were around before cell phones? I was, and let me tell you the ability to communicate was very, very different. I had to send written letters in the mail and by the time I received one back I had forgotten what I had written in my original letter to prompt the response. I remember my first car, a '74 Chevy Nova, stalling on the side of the road and my having to go knock on the closest house's door to ask to use their phone. Any time I needed to "research" something, I had to go to the library and use their card catalog system which took *forever* and when I wanted to look up old news articles, I needed to scroll through microfiche. (How many of you even know what that is?) When traveling long distances in a car, you could use a CB radio to communicate to the cars within a certain mile radius. And my first cell phone? It was attached to a receiver the size of a PS4. That is no joke. Ahhh . . . the '80s.

Now the world looks a whole lot different. Communication to the other side of the world can happen within seconds. And information is coming at us so fast that Twitter needed to be created so we could talk about it even faster. One of the technologies I adore the most is the ability to see the person I'm communicating with. It makes it seem like we are in the same room and is ideal for showing people what I'm talking about. Remember me telling you I'm a visual learner? Well, using communication platforms like Skype or Facetime allow me to learn visually quite seamlessly.

USING **SOCIAL MEDIA.**

Social media is a really big deal. I'm sure you've heard that before—and you may even believe it—but, be honest, are you overwhelmed by how fast it's moving and evolving? I feel your pain. The good news is that it closes the gap on having to wait . . . for anything. The bad news is since everything posts in real time, it's tough to "take it back" if you didn't mean it. Too many people see what you put out on the Internet even if the thing you regret posting gets deleted.

Regardless of how you feel about it, social media is here to stay and, in branding, if you want to make moo-lah you need to know where your customer is and hang out in the same sandbox they're hanging out in. That means if your audience is on Facebook, you need to be on Facebook. If they are on Twitter, you need to be on Twitter, and so on. Social media really is one of the most powerful tools in your marketing toolbox. If you know what you are doing, you can create a strong personal connection with your prospective customers. But, you need a plan—one built on a clear strategy. We'll talk more about marketing plans in the next chapter, but suffice it to say, you need to build a social media *strategy* into your marketing plan. Try to think about the following as you put one together.

Listen. Try to locate where your customers are hanging out and assess their social activities. Try to find small, focused audiences that align with your messages.

Plan. Define your social media objectives based upon your business plan. Determine how your brand's strength can be extended online.

Strategize. What will be your engagement process, and how often will you post? How do you plan to create relationships with consumers online? Who on your team will be leading this effort?

GETTING **LINKEDIN.**

We'll spend a bit of time talking about the importance of social media, but I want to spotlight LinkedIn because I have found it's one of the most effective business tools for personal brand exposure. The nice thing about LinkedIn is that it is designed for business professionals, so there are rules of engagement. LinkedIn is more pragmatic in its information delivery; whereas, some of the other social media platforms allows for more free-flow personal opinion.

LinkedIn is one of the most important social media platforms you should manage on a regular basis. It's your "professional" version of all social platforms, so it is paramount that it is updated regularly and reflects you as a business professional.

LinkedIn recommends we do a handful of things to ensure a solid and relevant profile:

1. Be authentic.
2. Create a distinctive profile headline.
3. Avoid clichés.
4. Be visible.
5. Build brand associations.
6. Add to your knowledge.
7. Share in LinkedIn Groups.
8. Be personal.
9. Be consistent.[22]

Don't forget to build your business page, as well. If you own a business, the two will go hand in hand until you move to the next business, so be mindful of how you brand that page. Focus on what's relevant for the company and of value to the audience.

...AND **EVERYTHING ELSE.**

LinkedIn, important though it is, presents only one of many social media platforms to use for personal branding. Here is a list of places to be and things to do online that online marketing experts recommend considering:

- Twitter
- Facebook
- Operate and write a blog
- Be a guest blogger on someone else's blog
- Participate in discussion groups
- Create and maintain a website with links that help with search engine optimization (SEO) and search engine marketing (SEM)
- Post about your work and work projects online
- Join and contribute to professional groups through LinkedIn

Remember our dreaded chapter 2—the one where I said if you couldn't get through it lovingly, it's probably best to gift **MOO-LAH-GY** to a friend? Well, here is where it rears its ugly head again, but hopefully the work is well underway so this won't freak you out. This is where doing a bit of that work comes in handy.

In order to build a communications strategy, you need to:

- Understand your goals.
- Create measurable objectives.
  (Remember the SMART strategy?)
- Characterize your customer.
  Identify their persona(s).
- Look at the competition.
- Develop your messages based upon your differentiators and positioning.

Sound familiar? Good for you for recognizing it. Next, you need to choose your communications channels. Remember, not all social media platforms are the same—and you need to not only pick the ones where your audience hangs out, you need to understand their engagement. There isn't a cookie-cutter process for making this choice. It takes thought. It takes a strategic point of view, which is why I'm always so shocked when I hear major corporations utilize interns or support staff to run their social media execution. The challenge is that, since it's happening in real time, you need to respond quickly or you will miss your window of opportunity. Responding in real time requires experience and good judgement because social media is permanent and when something is misstated or misinterpreted or simply wrong, damage control may be necessary.

How many of you remember the 2013 Super Bowl? If you do, you may remember the power went out and the entire stadium was in the dark. In real time, the marketing team behind Oreo cookies posted a tweet that was seen and heard around the world. Someone in their camp created a designed post that read, "Power out? No problem. You can still dunk in the dark." It was one of the most impressive examples of how social media should, and has, worked. It's in these glorious moments that magic happens, but you have to be at the ready to see it, respond to it, or better yet, originate it.

Finally, build a content strategy that covers the platforms you want to cover. Your list will be commensurate with your overall communication plan. Some of the areas to focus on are:

- Social media
- Email marketing
- Print media and direct mail
- Websites
- Video
- Public Relations
- Blogs
- Mobile device communications

Your plan should deliver engaging material and needs to align with your overall messaging. Consider the subject matter. It should only be product or service related. Remember, you want to position yourself as a thought leader. Post things that entertain, educate, and inform in each area of your expertise. And don't forget the Marketing Rule of 7. Try to re-purpose your content as many times as you can, but give it a slightly different perspective to keep it fresh and keep it relevant.

BRANDING VS. MARKETING.

Is what you're doing branding or is it marketing? Often, the terms branding, marketing, logo, and advertising are used interchangeably—but they aren't the same. They're not even close to the same, but they do support each other. Here's a visual of how they interconnect. All your branding and marketing must be done with the customer in mind. Your marketing and branding efforts work together, hand in hand, and your advertising and logos are elements of your marketing and branding.

Let's take a look at some examples where marketing and branding overlap:

>**Marketing:** Who will you sell to (audience); who is most likely to buy your offering (target); how are you different from competitors (value proposition); and why does your customer care (big idea)?

>**Branding:** How do you want your customer to feel when they interact with your company; what is your organization's mission, how do you describe your business' personality; and how do you indicate what makes you different from your competitors through words and pictures?

Your logo is used on marketing and communication materials, on your website, and on your business card, but it—in and of itself—is not considered marketing. It's part of your brand identity (which we covered in chapter 4).

Advertising should include your logo and can have a branding objective. Think of the billboard campaign for Snapchat. Have you seen it? The only thing on the billboard is the logo—there's nothing else. In that scenario, the objective of the billboard is to reinforce the brand. The billboard is advertising, and the logo is the tool to meet the branding objective. My son can pick this billboard out from a mile away; as a matter of fact, he was the one who pointed it out to me as we were speeding down the freeway. That's intentional and brilliantly played on the company's part.

Advertising can also have another marketing objective: sales. When you promote ticket sales to an event online, you are using advertising (tool) to market (sell) your event online. Your event is designed to create an experience (marketing) that your customers will remember (brand). Whew!

As I've mentioned, I'm a visual learner. I'm sure you can tell by how this book has been designed. And, as such, I thought it would be helpful for you to see a chart looking at all three side by side.

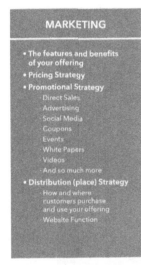

MARKETING	BRANDING	ADVERTISING
• The features and benefits of your offering	• Who you want to be and why	• Radio & T.V.
• Pricing Strategy	• The emotions you want customers to have	• Print: Magazine & Newspaper
• Promotional Strategy	• How you're different	• Billboards
· Direct Sales	• Visual Elements	• Non-Traditional
· Advertising	· Logo/Mark	• Online (paid)
· Social Media	· Tagline	· Facebook
· Coupons	· Colors	· LinkedIn
· Events	· Website Design	· Twitter
· White Papers	• Collateral	· Google
· Videos	· Business Cards	· Sponsored Content
· And so much more	· Letterhead	
• Distribution (place) Strategy	· Flyers, Brochures, & More	
· How and where customers purchase and use your offering	• Social Media	
· Website Function	· Facebook and LinkedIn Profiles	

But what happens when you boil branding and marketing down to their basic differences? At the bottom line, branding is visceral while marketing is tactile. It's a business trying to make an emotional connection (brand) through specific initiatives (marketing). Is this all starting to make sense? Wheaties had a campaign for many years that included their cereal boxes claiming it was "the breakfast of champions" (brand) which gave us the impression that if we ate them, we would be strong and we would be winners. They spotlighted Olympic athletes on the cover (marketing).

Branding is **why.**	Marketing is **how.**
Branding is **long-term.**	Marketing is **short-term.**
Branding is **macro.**	Marketing is **micro.**
Branding defines **trajectory.**	Marketing defines **tactics.**
Branding drives **enduring reputation.**	Marketing drives **periodic sales.**
Branding is the **reason someone buys.**	Marketing is the **reason someone thought to buy in the first place.**
Branding **builds loyalty.**	Marketing **generates response.**
Branding **creates value.**	Marketing **extracts value.**
Branding is the **being.**	Marketing is the **doing.**[23]

Let's look at one of the most recognized brands in coffee, Starbucks, and how they apply all three: branding, marketing, and advertising.

STARBUCKS AND BRANDING

Starbucks has positioned themselves as an influencer in the coffee space. Their intention is two-fold: they want you to go to work every day and share a cup of coffee with a friend, and they want to make the world a better place. From the beginning, they set out to be a different kind of company; one that not only celebrated coffee and a rich tradition, but one that also evoked a feeling of connection. Their logo, color palette, and store environment all speak to the brand's mission, their products have fun names, and they've invested a ton of money in packaging and branded products for sale.

STARBUCKS AND MARKETING

Starbucks offers numerous drinks and food, and they remember your name. They even offer the Starbucks Reserve Roastery & Tasting Room, in Seattle, the home of Starbucks. They've got the Starbucks Reward Program and they're big promoters of environmental efforts focused on reducing and reusing trash. They offer seasonal discounts and reward points, and implement huge social media outreach campaigns. In 2014, Starbucks launched its first brand campaign called, "Meet me at Starbucks."[24]

STARBUCKS AND ADVERTISING

Starbucks has a large advertising budget, placing ads wherever their clients are—including a heavy print campaign in magazines, TV commercials, billboards, and social media. Their ads are designed to reinforce their brand and to encourage customers to visit their stores, purchase product, and share experiences.

Let's bring this discussion down to the relationship level. The two scenarios that follow illustrate the importance of relationship in both branding and marketing.[25]

> **Scenario A:** You call up your friend and ask them to come over because you're selling Javita coffee and you want them to try it to see if they like it enough to buy it. Most likely, your friend will feel you were only interested in making a deal; that you (the brand) don't really care for them, their feelings, or their experience because you're clearly placing your product and profit before your relationship with them.

> **Scenario B:** You ask your friend to come over for a cup of coffee because you want to visit with them, engage in conversation, and enjoy some warm and cozy time together. You happen to be serving Javita coffee—a product line you sell. In this instance, you're making the relationship between you, and how your friend will feel when they engage with you, more sincere (brand).

In the second scenario, when the friend (the customer) sees the coffee (the product) other places he or she will be more likely to purchase it because the experience (your brand) will come to his or her mind.

I would be remiss if I didn't caution you that marketing and branding require resources. Even the much used "free eBook" promotion—an effective way to engage your audience and build your brand—is not free to the creator. Therefore, it's important to have the foresight to budget and save for the branding your company deserves.

Speaking of budgets. How do you know what you'll need? Well, first you need a list. Here are a few things to consider that we've already covered, which I'm going to reiterate:

- Pay for design.
- Get professional photography.
- Budget for targeted sales materials, internal communication, and training.
- Plan for marketing activities that may include promotions or advertising.
- Keep in mind you'll need to plan for a re-Fresh or re-Brand in approximately three years.

LIVE YOUR BRAND.

When you defined your brand, you made a promise to your customer. Are you keeping that promise? When businesses falter in keeping their promises they lose their customers' trust and their brands and businesses suffer. Living your brand throughout your business is an essential step in maintaining a loyal client base. If you don't do that, you don't make moo-lah.

My friends over at Woodchuck USA live their brand every second of every day. They manufacture wood products, and their mission is to bring nature back to people. This team is outside every day, exploring every facet of nature by skydiving, scuba diving, hiking, camping, and traveling the globe to explore, learn, and enjoy—and they give back to the earth by planting a tree for every wood product they sell. Their products are handmade in America by a staff that believes in their mission. Their products speak to their brand, and their staff does, too.

BRAND **STRATEGY.**

Customers need you to define your brand well because they need brands—and the promises they convey—to help them to make purchasing decisions in an environment where they can become exhausted with all the options. If the customer trusts your brand they'll pay for it and worry about the details later. Developing a brand is like developing any other relationship: it's built on trust, and just like in any relationship brand trust takes time to build.

You have a brand right now, whether you've launched your business or not. Because your brand stands in for you when you're not there, building a specific brand must be high on your priority list. Why should you care about your brand? If time is money, brand earns you both time and money. Here's how.

A STITCH IN TIME.

Brand, done well, does two things:

First, it saves you time when making future decisions because you've done the strategic thinking up front. The clarity you achieved through the brand definition stage will allow you to make the most of your decisions when you translate and live your brand with your customers, employees, and partners.

Second, a strong brand will also bring more qualified prospects to your door, saving you the time it takes to weed out clients that aren't a good fit. Your brand communicates who you are before you even see the client. Your logo, colors, website, business cards—some of the elements of your brand—allow current clients to introduce you to new prospects. If your brand elements don't inspire confidence from your customer they will hesitate to refer you. But, if they do inspire confidence, you're already a step ahead with new clients.

A BIT MORE MOO-LAH.

Brands make you moo-lah. Loyal customers will pay a 20-30% price premium for brands they love.[26] Let's take the difference between McDonald's and Burger King, for instance. Both sell essentially the same things: meat, cheese, bread, and beverages. However, in 2012 the difference in sales between McDonald's and Burger King was $27 billion in McDonald's favor—all due to branding.[27] Using the same example, assuming we are spending somewhere in the neighborhood of 1/1 millionth of the branding premium in our brand budget, that could represent a $27,000 difference in sales between you and your closest competitor, all due to the power of brand. What could you do with an extra $27,000 in your budget (or your pocket) per year?

SO WHAT?

This chapter was chock full of discussion around communication and the importance of getting your point across with the least amount of consumer confusion. Helping to overcome objections by attacking them head on is important. How do you do that? By making the connection between what you do and how it will change a consumer's life seamless. Getting the "yes" is all about eliminating the "no." Remember: a "no" is simply a pause caused by misunderstanding or general confusion. Getting a "yes" makes you moo-lah, and it's through multiple marketing channels—social media being one of the biggest, easiest, and quickest—that you tell people what you have going on and how what you sell can solve their problem. But, you need a plan. Putting together a plan helps you hit it out of the park the first time, freeing you up to hit another one, and so on. Remember, communication—the right communication—is vital.

BRAND BITS.

- A successful business takes strategy.
- Eight out of ten businesses fail.
- A "yes" equates to a sale.
- Know your big idea.
- Legally protect your business name.
- Create stories around your brand.
- Communication may be immediate, but is also permanent.
- Social media is one of the most powerful marketing tools.
- Branding is visceral. Marketing is tactile.
- A strong brand connects the dots, turning a "no" into a "yes."

CHAPTER **SIX**

WHERE THE RUBBER HITS THE ROAD.

"THE" PLAN IS NOT A FOUR LETTER WORD.

If I had a nickel for every time I've heard "I don't have a plan" over the years, I'd be a really wealthy gal. I've stopped asking why there isn't a plan because I've learned not everyone is a planner, not to mention—have you read chapter 2? If you don't like heady stuff, the plan finds itself at the bottom of the to-do list.

When I'm having my initial conversation with a potential client, the reason I ask about his or her plan is not to get the nickel, but to get some answers to help me formulate my advice. I need to know their overall goals and objectives because I need to figure out how we are going to achieve those goals. Maybe we don't need to re-Brand. Maybe we don't even need to increase the brand's current social media effort. It all depends on those goals and objectives.

And, of course, there are two kinds of plans. The business plan is "the plan" with the established goals and objectives. The marketing plan is the vehicle to get there. If I'm talking to someone who doesn't have either, it could be a much longer road.

When I was selling homes, my pay was 100% commission based. I did not have a salary, nor was there any kind of guarantee on how much money I would make in any given timeframe. I had to sell a home to collect a paycheck. If I didn't kill it, I didn't eat. Living in a winter climate, where building homes is a cyclical business, I knew I needed to be proactive if I was to guarantee against a hungry month. My overall plan was simple: I knew how much money I wanted to make in a year's time, so I took that number and divided it by twelve months. That indicated how many homes I needed to sell each month (because I knew the average price my homes were selling for and I knew my fixed commission rate). But, I also knew there were certain months during the year when I would have very few sales. For instance, summer was a difficult time to sell homes because families were making the most of the nice weather and spending free time with their families or on vacation. I also knew my builder would offer deeper incentives during certain times of the year to reduce carrying costs (the cost of having standing inventory that carried over into another month). My plan accounted for those variable situations. I had to sell more homes in the better months and accept there would be only the occasional sale in the slower ones. Anticipating how the year would look gave me the energy to stay the course when it was crazy busy and cut myself some slack when times were slow.

Having a plan kept me sane during both the high highs and low lows of the industry. However, the initial plan or intention wasn't enough. I needed to execute an initiative that would drive people into my model home and provide some kind of incentive for them to buy. Now keep in mind, in my environment, I did not have the luxury of being mobile like an existing real estate agent. I was landlocked, meaning I had to wait until someone literally came to me. I couldn't leave the building.

How do you get people to cross your threshold? How do you draw traffic to you? A marketing plan.

MARKETING PLAN.

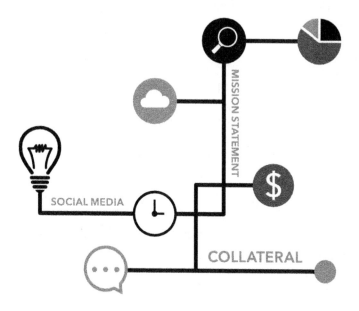

A marketing plan can consist of anywhere from a handful to several hundred pages. What determines the number? How much initiative will it take for you to reach your business goals and how wide do you need to cast your net to reach your target audience? Fish where there are fish, right? So, if the right fish are in a variety of ponds, you need to get your boat into each body of water. Regardless of how big the marketing plan becomes, you'll definitely want it to cover one year's worth of time and you'll want it to include several sections, including:

EXECUTIVE SUMMARY
(mission statement)

TARGET CUSTOMERS
(personas)

UNIQUE SELLING PROPOSITION
(value proposition)

POSITIONING STRATEGY
(you versus the competition)

DISTRIBUTION PLAN
(how your customers will acquire your product or service)

YOUR OFFERS
(what you sell)

MARKETING MATERIALS
(collateral)

PROMOTIONS STRATEGY
(incentives to purchase)

ONLINE MARKETING STRATEGY
(social media)

CONVERSION STRATEGY
(how you will get your customer to say yes)

JOINT VENTURES AND PARTNERSHIPS
(form an alliance with another enterprise)

REFERRAL STRATEGY
(affiliates and the like)

STRATEGY FOR INCREASING PRICES
(how much and how frequent)

RETENTION STRATEGY
(repeat customers)

FINANCIAL PROJECTIONS
(budgets and expenditures)[28]

 Does some of this list sound familiar? Yep—the dreaded chapter 2. Not everything was covered in that chapter (or in this book), because I am only addressing the sections related to building a strong brand, but I wanted to include them in the list because, as you continue to build your plan, you will need to consider them as part of your overall marketing plan.

Keep in mind a marketing plan should not be carved in stone. It needs to have some fluidity to it so you can add or subtract based upon what the market is telling you. It's the litmus test for what works and what doesn't during the year. It serves as a system of checks and balances to measure against your business plan to make sure your bases are covered in trying to hit your goals.

So, remember how I had to figure out how to get people to come to me when I was selling homes? Well, selling your products and/or services isn't really any different, since so much of it is based in getting your product in front of buyers. That's where online marketing starts to feel awfully familiar—though way more effective—than how I did my marketing almost two decades ago with my feet on the ground without the benefit of today's technology. Even with new technology, the actual process of "getting the word out" hasn't changed much over time. Let's take a look.

NETWORKING.

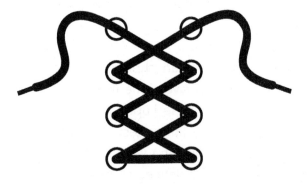

I first became aware of the power of networking back in high school in the '80's, but not for the reasons you'd think. It happened because of my brother, my only sibling. I was three grades older than him and he had a tough run in school. He had been diagnosed early on with ADHD and couldn't take any drugs due to the severe reactions he had to the medication. Having ADHD back in the '80's labeled him as an outcast especially since he couldn't benefit from medicine and as a result he grappled with being bullied; not only from school children, but from adults as well. There was a time when he was in second grade where he was ridiculed by his teacher for having shoes with untied laces. He always had one or both shoes untied. The teacher called my brother to the front of the classroom and instructed the students to chant, "Cry baby! Cry baby!" and proceeded to tie my brother's shoe laces into a million knots. Knots my mother had to then remove for hours with a fork. This bullying continued through his early school years as well as through high school where he walked to and from school because he was teased mercilessly when he rode the bus. Cruel actions from others didn't deter his compassion in helping others especially those with disabilities; however that kindness was rarely reciprocated. I watched as my brother was teased and punished and I hated it. I feared for him. I feared once I graduated, he would have three more years without me. And then, it hit me. I was friends with many juniors. So, I reached out to the ones I'd become friends with and I asked them a favor. The favor was to watch out for my little brother. They responded with, "we've got his back." I was able to graduate with some relief knowing there were eyes on my brother... even if it was for only a year until my junior friends graduated. You see, networking is first and foremost about relationships. You have to lead with that or your efforts will be for naught. I had established trusted relationships with people that were a grade below me. I respected them and they respected me. It was a respect that was earned and a direct reflection of my personal brand and how I represented myself, so I felt comfortable in asking this favor that meant everything to me and no value to them. Networking in this case started well before the ask. It happened organically and I didn't even know it... until I needed it to work. You might argue this example isn't a true form of "networking", but it is because in my mind, networking is the by-product of strong relationships with people and the give and take both personally and professionally that happens as a result of those relationships. The moral of this story is you never know who might be the person who could lend you a hand in a time of need, so be open to meeting and getting to know as many people as you can. Get to really know them and be sure it comes from a place of giving first. I've met people who only wanted to know me because they wanted something from me. I look at them very differently as a result and it casts a negative shadow on their personal brand in my eyes. It's tough to recover from that perception, so authenticity is salient. I actually share a story about this very thing next.

Three decades ago, eye contact and a handshake meant something. Relationship building was a real and richly fulfilling thing. Believe it or not, it still means something today even though we now live in a digital world. I think it's the digital part that gets most of us in trouble because nothing can replace meeting face to face—even if it's virtual (which is why I love Facetime and Skype and any other platform that allows you to communicate visually over long distances). It just makes a huge difference to see and "feel" the expressions of the people you're talking to. Remember, brand is a three part equation: image, voice, and promise. To get to know someone on a 3-dimensional level allows you to really "get to know them" and it speeds up the process.

The power of networking is unsurpassed, in converting sales in my opinion. And, I'm certain you recognize its importance as well—but how much of it are you doing monthly, weekly, or even daily? Is it enough? Have you made networking part of your marketing plan? If not, you should. I came to that realization on January 1, 2008. I woke up that day and had an epiphany. I thought to myself, *"I have lived in Minneapolis my whole life and if everyone on the planet has six degrees of separation, for sure they are two degrees of separation in this town."* That was a shocking reality for me. I had been so busy in my career, I never took the time to look up and get to know the people in my own backyard. So, I went on a quest. I was determined to meet and get to know as many people as I could and so I embarked upon what some have said was a bit of looney tunes. I reached out to everyone locally I was connected with on LinkedIn and asked them if they would be interested in meeting for coffee. To my surprise, 100% agreed and connected me to several people... and so on. I was well on my way to what were the most profound networking experiences of my life. I met with three to five people per day and I did so for four to seven days a week. Consistently. For 18 months. During those visits I saw the generosity of people and their willingness to give me a spot of their time which is such a precious gift. These people had busy lives, full-time jobs, and other demands, yet they agreed to give me 30 minutes of their time. I was beyond humbled and determined I would do the same. I would commit to giving my time to those who needed it. Through the experience, not only did I meet amazingly interesting people, I established what will be many lifelong friendships. Friendships that are reciprocal. Friendships that when you send an email with the subject line: *"I need your help"* the response is immediate with, *"Absolutely. What can I do?"* That is the true power of networking.

LEVEL OF ENGAGEMENT.

Let's take my home building example a step further. When you staff a model home as a real estate agent, you're not allowed to operate as a traditional Realtor, so you can't put people in their cars and take them to other properties to view. Instead, you spend your days waiting for someone to visit the model home and, often, you can feel apprehensive in asking them to purchase once they do finally arrive. When I was a sales manager, it was my job to get my team to engage each and every person who came through the door of our model homes. Whenever complacency set in—or an apprehension in asking for the sale—I reminded my team the person visiting their model home had gone out of their way to do so. I can think of a million things to do on a sunny Saturday afternoon other than go around looking at homes, but it's the only thing I want to do when I am in the market to buy one. Right? So the instructions to my team were simple: If someone crosses your threshold, they've given you permission to sell them a home. They're look-ing for one anyway; otherwise they wouldn't be there. There's nothing wrong with talking to the prospect—and "creating engagement"—when com-munication is so important anyway, right?

You can have that engagement both in person and virtually, but it's up to you to determine how deep the engagement will go. People buy from people and, if you're in business, you are in the relation-ship business, so figuring out what works for you is really important. This means it is important to get out and connect with as many people as you can, in a variety of ways, and build solid relationships so you can stay at the top of their minds and the people you contact will tell others about you.

Try not to pressure anyone for a sale right out of the gate, though. Build the relationship first, because—in the long run—that's what really counts. When you lead with trying to sell someone something (like our coffee example in chapter 5), your pitch comes off as disingenuous and offensive. I read an article in *Brand Quarterly* magazine that addressed "premature solicitation." The author shared a story about how he was about to take the stage and speak to an audience he had never met before when a gentleman from the audience approached him, introduced himself, and said, "Hi, it is a real pleasure to meet you. I understand you know Richard Branson. I offer specialized marketing services and I am sure his Virgin enterprises could benefit from what I provide. Could you please introduce me to him so I can show him how this would assist his companies?"

What do you think he said? What he said in his head (not out loud) was: "Are you completely insane? I'm going to introduce you, someone I don't know and don't have any relationship with, to Sir Richard, whom I've only met a few times, so that you can proceed to attempt to sell him a product or service that I don't know anything about and haven't used myself? Yeah, right. That's NEVER going to happen."[29]

I recently had the pleasure of meeting Paul the loveliest older gentleman who is on his fourth career. He is currently mentoring entrepreneurs and startups in Minneapolis. When we met, he had a portfolio several pages deep of success stories, and he told me the role he occupies when assisting is CEO/COO. That role often needs to be a bit more tough love than anything else.

I was in a meeting with him as his co-mentor for the startup company I mentioned in chapter 1 who had made it as a semi-finalist in an entrepreneurial contest in Minnesota, which looks for the next breakthrough idea. We were assigned to this team and were instructed to help them with their semi-finalist entry on a really tight deadline. Instead of digging right in—which was my first inclination—his first thirty minutes with the CEO of the startup was spent asking this young man about his life, his aspirations, his family, and his dreams.

It was immensely powerful and humbling from the eyes of a "brand girl" who has been referred to a time or two as Darth Vader due to my no-nonsense, all-business approach to doing the work. He took the time to really get to know this person before he launched into giving his advice. It was absolutely lovely, an immeasurable icebreaker, and I will remember it always. I learned a huge lesson that day and I wish to pass it onto you: really get to know the person you are talking with so you can move to a place of empathy before moving forward together.

EVENTS.

I'm sure you've attended numerous events—possibly even the same one over and over (in the case of an annual convention)—and you've collected materials, taken notes, asked for business cards, and had conversations over lunch. Maybe you've even hosted an event or been an exhibitor at an event where all of the above still applies. Do you feel you've optimized those opportunities? Did you convert sales as a result of attending? Or, better yet, do you feel you made moo-lah as a result of the event in question?

Event marketing is one of the fastest growing fields in marketing and advertising today. Events are everywhere—just check your Facebook events calendar, your email inbox, or your LinkedIn feed to see how many are available to attend. There are local, regional, and national opportunities. So, how do you choose whether or not to attend? How do you decide which events you'll attend and which you'll pass over? Maybe a bigger question is, why are there so many events anyway? There are certainly more than ever. Wouldn't you say?

WHY IS EVENT ATTENDANCE IMPORTANT?

First, today's discriminating buyers want more than an advertising pitch when making buying decisions. They want to establish relationships with the person they are buying from. They need proof the product works (proof of concept) and they need to hear people talking about how great it is so the product or service being sold has merit and relevancy for them (social proof). Events offer a unique opportunity for buyers to interact with brands to get a firsthand sense of the (selling) company's philosophy, perspective, and personality. Event marketing is a necessity as it has become an integral part of the demand of the consumer and can impact a company's bottom line.

THE THREE SIDES TO THE
EVENT TRIANGLE.

There are three areas of events and tradeshows you'll want to focus on. You need to go into the event prepared, having done some homework, so you know what you are walking into and you can tee up opportunities before you even arrive. During the event is when the rubber hits the road. You've got to work it the whole time you are there. Remember that each event is costing you moo-lah, whether in physical dollars or your precious time away from the office (or both), so it needs to be fruitful. Finally, the post-event time is critical in closing loops and continuing the conversation—not to mention a great chance to convert leads into buyers because I promise you few in attendance will do any real "post" effort!

Let's take a quick peek at the players at every event:

- **Attendee**–a person going to an event as a participant

- **Exhibitor**–a person at an event as a tradeshow participant

- **Producer**–a person planning and executing an event as the host

Focusing on these players as your core sales opportunities, we can really distill down the opportunities to monetize and create impact. As I mentioned above, making the most of the event holistically will certainly pay off. Let's dig deeper.

In order to help you understand the value and impact of event marketing, you first need to understand the power of experiential marketing.

EXPERIENTIAL MARKETING.

Remember my friend, Dave from chapter 1? He shared a story with me about a client experience the agency he worked for created in 2010. The client was Forever 21 and they launched an innovative billboard campaign that would live in Times Square in New York City—amid the noisy, visually stimulating overload of media competing for market share. The agency came up with an interactive campaign that involved the people on the street and they did it using real time snapshots of those people who stopped to watch the billboard interact with its audience. They created software that allowed a digital billboard to interact with the

passers-by on the street. The two-dimensional models in the billboard "play" with people walking along the streets. They choose people from the crowd, pick them up, and either toss them around like dolls, kiss them and turn them into frogs, or put them in their purses and walk away.

29%
increase in average time spent with a billboard

375k
people visiting the board each week

3
million media impressions

Ingenious, right? You have no idea. It's been such a hit, that the city of New York contacted Forever 21 and their agency, asking them to move their camera up onto the sidewalk as it was pointed toward the busy streets and people had become so enamored of (and wanted to play with) the billboard, they were causing traffic jams.

So, what was happening with this billboard and the people walking by? They were having an experience—all done through marketing. The Forever 21 billboard experience is an event, but it's done so cleverly that many don't even realize it.

When was the last time you were in a movie theater? Personally, I go often. Recently, I went to a matinee to see one of the latest releases to break up my day. I had two choices, the regular theater or the 3D experience. I chose the regular experience, and between previews the theater had an advertising campaign that said "Experience it at IMAX theaters." I thought, "What is the IMAX experience?" As soon as I got home, I checked it out and learned, in a nutshell, the IMAX experience is like no other movie experience. What I determined from their website is the people behind IMAX think it's important that something as simple as a movie should be more like an event. They want it to be an experiential event. And they are focused on finding ways to take that experience to another level.

Their tagline is: "IMAX is Believing." Exploring further through their website, I realized what that means. It means when you go into a theater, you lose yourself in the movie and forget you're even there. You are sitting in a dark theater surrounded by other people you don't know, staring at a screen, but convinced you're somewhere else. Have you experienced that?[30]

So, we've reviewed a walk through Times Square looking at advertising and attending a movie each as "events," but how about something else seemingly less consequential, but no less an event?

Check out this CLIF Bar box. Their packaging is filled with information on how you can (and should) take an adventure—an event. Even our snacks want us to have an experience! In this case, CLIF Bars wants you to record your adventures and post them for the world to see.

Even something as simple as a gift card can be an experience. Take Giftly for example. You can give Giftly gift cards electronically or by mail and the recipients are asked to share a photo of what they purchased and where they spent it, and to post the experience on social media.

So how does all of this apply to event marketing? In the Forever 21 example passers-by are encouraged to participate in the interactive event. With our movie example, movie executives want us to get lost in the experience of the film. In the case of the CLIF bar example, they desire you have an experience while you eat your bar. With Giftly, they want you to use their gift card to have an experience. And, experiences are events. CLIF and Giftly chose to market their products and tie them back to an event. Make sense? "The trick to pulling off an effective event marketing campaign is to identify the target audience correctly and create an experience that remains in participants' memories. By finding an opportunity to interact with the right demographic of people—both current customers and prospective buyers—a brand can build favorable impressions and long-lasting relationships. The best, most creative events create interactions that not only reflect positively on the brand at the time, but generate a buzz long after the event is over"[31]—not to mention the potential sales from those who attended, as well as those who only heard the aftershocks.

HOW TO MAKE EVENTS WORK FOR **YOUR BUSINESS.**

When considering adding an event to your marketing plan, you need to decide what the overarching goal of the event is for you and your business. Will you be there to launch or talk about a new product? Is your primary goal to build personal relationships with certain attendees or speakers? Are you hoping to learn about the scheduled content? Maybe you're going so you can build brand loyalty and gain brand exposure, or gain insight on new ideas to implement in your own business. Regardless of the reason(s), you need to be clear on the event objective before you go so you can decide to get involved from a pragmatic standpoint, instead of an emotional one.

Make a master list of the goals you wish to achieve before committing to an event. I call mine an "action plan" because, to me, the items on the list are more than goals, they are "have-to-do's." As you plan for the event, consider: Are your goals realistic? Can you reach them? If you don't think you can, is that okay? Plan to stay focused on those goals throughout the process (from pre- to post-event) to ensure a higher probability of success in achieving them.

Let me give you an example of where this planning has worked for me. I chose to be an exhibitor at one of the largest children's products shows in the nation with the goal of building brand awareness around my children's educational product, Bye Bye Monster and to see if I could meet Jenny McCarthy. I knew she would be there launching her Too Good organic children's bedding line. Because I was planning to have others who could staff my booth, and had the event schedule ahead of time, I knew when she would be there and planned coverage at my booth so I could sneak away to go listen to her presentation. I didn't realize the presentation was for media only until I arrived, but I took the bull by the horns and walked past security as though I was a member of the media. Fortunately, it worked. The only seat remaining was in the front row, so I took it—even though the presentation had already begun and I had to walk past all the seated listeners. But, I stayed focused on my goal, and once the presentation wrapped and the Q&A session was over, Jenny agreed to take pictures with a handful of people. I was third in line. Make no mistake—I seized the moment and handed her a sample of Bye Bye Germs (a sister product to Bye Bye Monster), my all natural, anti-viral hand sanitizer and suggested she use it since she had so many hands to shake. (I chose that product because I knew it was the most relevant in my lineup under the circumstances.) To make a long story short, she told me she'd have her assistant call me (which she did) and I was flown out to Los Angeles, met with her and her team, and was asked to create a private label, anti-viral spray which was included in her tradeshow event swag the following year. None of this would have happened if I'd allowed myself to become flustered or sidetracked along the way. My goals were very clear ahead of time and, as a result, my intentions were purposeful and I came out successful.

Obviously, my goals as an exhibitor were very specific in that role and at that event. Fortunately, I achieved what I set out to do. But, there was a cost attached to it (exhibitor's fees, staffing costs, travel, etc.) and I have found the cost of going to events is commensurate with the role you play (ie: attendee, exhibitor, producer) in that there are different fees and different goals attached to each role.

ATTENDEE.

When you are planning to attend an event, you want to do your homework. In order for you to reach your goals through your action plan, you need to do some front-end legwork. Here are some things to consider:

- How many years has the event taken place (consider the strength of the event is mirrored in its attendance level)?

- What was the general attendee feedback about the outcomes of the previous years (is it a good event or not)?

- Do you know anything about the speakers (do they have something to offer that will serve you and/or your business)?

- What do you know about your fellow attendees (are they the right demographic to help you reach your goals)?

- What type of crowd they are trying to draw (how will the attendees' views align to you and your goals)?

As you consider these questions before attending, you're looking for answers that will both help you determine if you think you can monetize and reach your goals as a result of this event and also will guide you in putting together a successful action plan to achieve those goals. If part of your goal list is to procure one client, how are you going to go about doing so? Having some of your questions answered ahead of time will put you in a better position of getting in front of the right people, enabling you to have the ideal conversations that could turn into business.

Let's assume you've done your reconnaissance and you've decided to attend the event. Your research has determined this is the right event for you, so you'll have to make sure you can justify the attendance fee. Before you move forward, next you'll want to put together an event budget. But the event budget goes beyond what the price of admission is to attend—there are other expenses involved. Let's take a look at a hypothetical scenario:

> You are attending a three-day international conference where there will be upwards of 1,500 people in attendance. The attendees are all members of a woman's CEO organization and you are, too. Your goal is to

reconnect with old friends, listen to great content, and make as many connections as possible to build upon your network. What will being there cost you?

FLIGHT	$414
HOTEL (5 NIGHTS)	$745
MEALS	$490
TRANSPORTATION (TAXI)	$80
ATTENDANCE FEE	$495
BUSINESS CARDS	$75
OPPORTUNITY COSTS	$5,250
TOTAL:	**$7,549**

Let's break down some of these fees further; particularly the opportunity costs.

OPPORTUNITY COSTS.

"Opportunity cost" is a concept used in economics, which describes the value placed on a missed opportunity. In other words, this looks at what would happen if you were to stay home and do activities to create revenue, instead of doing the tasks necessary to attend your event (ie: research, shopping, scheduling travel, etc.). Remember: the hours you spend doing the latter prevent you from generating business during your prep time and your time away; therefore, this all counts as a potential missed opportunity.

How did I calculate "missed opportunities" in my scenario? Here is a quick formula for making a few assumptions—you can calculate your own based upon your own specific situation. So, we are assuming it will take you eight hours of work time to prep for the event (ie: to schedule travel, order extra business cards, make some calls to get logistics, etc.), ten hours of travel time (ie: to and from the airports, at the airports, in the air, and in ground transportation to and from the event), and twenty-four (business) hours while you are actually attending the event— assuming three eight-hour days. I used an arbitrary rate of $125/hour for this example. (You'll want to use your actual rate for this calculation.)

Opportunity costs:
8 prep hours + 10 travel hours + 24 event hours
= 42 total hours "lost"

42 lost hours x $125/hour
= $5,250 in opportunity costs

Looking back at our scenario, we are investing $7,549 in a three-day event. Is it worth it? Do you think you can recoup those dollars while you are there by generating future business? In my scenario, I felt I could—but you'll have to make that decision on a case-by-case basis. Consider this:

> **1.** You encounter 100 people and have substantive conversations with one third of them, or approximately thirty-three people.

2. Let's say, of those thirty-three people, you have the opportunity to continue the conversation once you are back home with, let's say, one third again. That's about eleven people—and those are sales calls you conduct the very next week.

3. And, let's say of those eleven people you actually convert one third of them within thirty days, so four people become clients.

This means not only did you make moo-lah on those four new clients within a month, you made 100 brand impressions. Many of those prospective consumers (if not all) will connect with you through some form of social media (LinkedIn, Facebook, or Twitter) and go to your website and add you to their database. You will do the same and have an opportunity to stay in front of all of them. Suddenly, they all become "warm" leads—and those are good odds.

EXHIBITOR.

I love exhibiting. It's one of my all-time favorite marketing efforts. I love it so much over the years I've made it a family affair by including my son in my exhibitor adventures. The biggest endeavor Joey and I undertook was as exhibitors at the Minnesota State Fair—an event that is not for the faint of heart. Exhibitors must work twelve-hour days for twelve days—in the hottest part of the summer—speaking to an average of 152,000 people per day. That's right. Over 1.8 million people attend the fair every year.[32] When planning for my exhibition, I knew people would be getting eaten alive by mosquitos once the sun went down, so we spotlighted our all-natural insect repellent, Bye Bye Bugs. It was a hit—we sold out each day.

There are numerous reasons to exhibit, so let's look at a few of them.

One of the most important reasons to exhibit at an event is, as an exhibitor, you have a captive audience—a group of people in attendance who are there to take in everything that is familiar as well as new at the fair. They try to see as much as they can and most spend the entire day walking around so the chances of them stopping by your booth is pretty high. When you have attendees at an event and there is exhibitor space, it is an encouraged (and expected) practice the attendees will walk through the exhibition space. Often, there are even incentives to do so, such as free giveaways, drawings, scavenger hunts, and the like. As an exhibitor, you have the attendees' attention—and it's your job to optimize those moments.

You also have the opportunity to be singularly focused. To capitalize on this, you should choose one thing to spotlight and "sell." Unfortunately, many exhibitors go "too wide" with their offerings, confusing and overwhelming the attendees, causing them to move on. By contrast, if you keep a finite goal in mind, you will be a refreshing sight to very sore eyes, and the likelihood of an attendee spending a lingering moment at your booth will go up exponentially.

And it's not just about you, as a person. When your booth components, display, and handout materials are well thought out, you can get huge brand recognition because many people aren't as thoughtful when putting together their booth spaces, and they don't take into consideration the booth's surroundings, event circumstances, traffic flow, and audience when planning their space and putting together their strategy.

PRODUCER.

 Before you decide to become an event producer, ask yourself one question: Do you have the resources (time, money, manpower, and connections) to execute an event on your own, or would you benefit from partnering with an established event? I've seen a ton of collaborative events where people and organizations teamed up and partnered together to produce them. You've heard the saying "It takes a village," right? Well, sometimes it's definitely beneficial to have the extra sets of hands. Even so, prior to teaming up with partners and/or sponsors be sure to research their brands and their corporate missions to confirm they align with your own. If they do—and you decide to move forward—be sure you each spell out

your goals, objectives, and expectations for the event well before committing to the partnership.

As you being to plan, you'll need to consider a lot of really specific logistics. They may not be glamorous, but they can make or break any event. For instance: What would be the best time of year to hold your event? Sometimes events are more conducive to a specific time of year—which can depend on your location, climate, and so forth. Research shows the best month to host an event is January followed by September, then October, March, April, June, November, February, May, July, December, and August respectively. So, you'll obviously want to avoid July, December, and August, because they are the bottom three months. Of course, that data is skewed if an event is specific to a season, such as the Minnesota State Fair—which only occurs at the end summer in August. Saturday has been found to be the best day of the week for most events, followed by Sunday, then Thursday, Wednesday, Tuesday, Friday, and Monday. (Basically, avoid Friday and Monday.) Also, you should try to avoid holidays or the day of any major sporting event like the Super Bowl, as well as any other major events going on in the area so you don't have to compete with it.[33]

QUESTIONS TO ASK.

Can you hold the event in your local area, or do you need to consider a venue and geography that will draw a bigger—or different—crowd? The annual eWomenNetwork Conference is always held in Dallas, Texas; however, the location of their "Platinum" event—which is smaller and can offer some variety—changes annually. The annual conference needs to be static as attendees come from around the globe, so they need to count on it year after year. An interesting thing to note: the eWomenNetwork conference is held in August—the worst month of the year for conferences. Want to know why? Because it's the least busy event time of the year for local venues, so eWomenNetwork can keep attendee costs low by bargaining for low hotel fees and the like, making the time of year a perk for its attendees.

Will you affiliate with a charity or sponsors? Sometimes it makes sense to do this and sometimes it doesn't. The decision is entirely up to you, and you need to make it based on your goals and objectives for the event.

Above all—as with any partnership—you'll want to make sure expectations are defined and met for both sides.

What are your plans for the media? Will they be included or not? How will you handle media involvement? Media exposure can certainly be nice to have; however, you need to make sure you also have media "handlers" so everything pertaining to any media in attendance is executed smoothly.

Should you have a themed event? Themes can be a great way to increase attendance—if used appropriately. I am involved with Children's Hospital and Clinics Minnesota Foundation, and many of their events are themed, giving attendees a reason to get dressed up and do something unexpected. But, themed events aren't for everyone, so give consideration to how complicated it will be to find the perfect outfit for your attendees. Will they have to invest a ton of moo-lah to pull "the look" together? Will they ever wear the outfit again? Does the theme tie into the mission of the event somehow so it will enhance the event because of the theme? Themed parties can certainly be fun and crafted in such a way it's affordable and realistic for people to attend.

Can you get a celebrity or expert spokesperson to be a keynote speaker? Believe it or not, celebrities can go a long way toward bringing up your attendance—if they are the right celebrity for the event and your intended audience. If you can get the right one, you should—especially if they will agree to do it for no charge (however, you might want to factor this into your budget as a cost, just in case). Sometimes you can kill two birds with one stone by securing a celebrity and offering to donate a percentage of your event proceeds to the charity of his or her choice. Then, you are able to support a charity and you have your headliner. But, choose your celebrity or expert wisely. You wouldn't want to bring in a country western singing group if the audience prefers rap. If your expert spokesperson has a strong political point of view and is quite vocal about it, that may alienate part of your audience who feels the opposite. Choose based upon the audience demographic. If there is a room full of young people, find someone who will resonate with them. If the audience is primarily women, consider someone who can speak from a place of experience to that gender. A disconnect will hurt you, so plan accordingly.

How will your company's brand be reinforced? You will want to make sure that every square inch of your event speaks to your brand—from the napkins, to the music piped into the room, to the speakers, to the swag. Be sure you police how your brand is being represented and promoted. If this is your event, it's going to be a direct reflection on you—whether that reflection is good or bad is up to you.

What is the event timetable and budget?

Planning committees can go a bit off the rails when it comes to these two things. Having a realistic timetable is crucial for event success—not to mention staff sanity. When you have unrealistic timeframes, you can get all tangled up in unmet deadlines, rush charges, and re-work. As we've discussed, re-work can get messy, so plan your event out and back into a calendar. Give yourself enough time to do a real budget plan. There are always unexpected fees that pop up and you want to make

sure you have a 15-25% buffer in your budget so that you don't go into shock. Do your due diligence and get out a calculator and open an Excel spreadsheet and run it like you would a profit and loss statement (P&L).

With any event, you have an opportunity to improve the user experience and leave your attendees feeling full and as excited as raving fans. How do you get that result? Think about your audience and what makes them tick, what gets them excited, and what their interests are and build on that. Lead with your audience. Remember, they are the only ones that matter since the event is for THEM. If you feed them with content and an experience worth paying for, they'll spread the word to others and come back again—either to that event or another you put on.

EVENT BRAND **MONITORING.**

So, we've explored the importance—and varia-
tions—of the roles you can take at events. Now
let's look at event-related brand "monitoring." As
you work your plan, network, and attend events,
you need to be listening—and learning. Learning
about what? About how people react and respond
to you, your product or service, and your brand.
Does it need tweaking? If so, there are three options for how you can tweak what you do: re-Fresh,
re-Brand, or re-Position.

During my years working for homebuilders, my
roles included marketing, sales, and management.
During my sales days, I was asked to take over
sales in a community in a small town where people
tended to live—and stay. Townspeople might leave
for college, but they generally came back and
raised their own families. I was selling "production

townhomes" (homes built with specific inclusions and add-on features aimed to keep the price point low). We were catering to entry-level and second-time buyers and, as with most production builders, many of the components of the home used materials sourced through contracts with our vendor partners—and the windows in these townhomes were no exception. You see, although this town was home to one of the most-recognized names in windows in the country, we had a window contract with a competitive window manufacturer. When people from the community would stop in, each would ask me "What windows are in these townhomes?" I couldn't tell them what they wanted to hear. Hearing that, these hometown prospects would push back and insist we change out all of the windows before they would agree to purchase.

This was the first time in my career I got a taste of the need for a "brand pivot." In this scenario, it came in the form of re-Positioning, as we needed to make an executive decision: Should we honor the vendor agreement and risk not selling any homes to anyone who grew up in the community, or should we make an exception and swap out the windows? We made the exception, swapped out the windows, and sold out quickly. The moral of the story is every one of us needs to be continually reviewing how our brand is being received—and how it impacts sales. If at any point it's hindering the latter, it needs to be addressed, but you need to look at it with a keen eye to know which to do: re-Fresh, re-Brand or re-Position.

Brands are constantly threatened by both external *and* internal factors. Because your brand can show up in so many ways at any event, you'll need a professional brand strategist to review things periodically to ensure the brand continues to stay relevant. Be careful not to avoid the signs or to simply duct tape things together until a later date. If you do that, your brand runs the risk of complete deterioration and duct tape will only hold for so long.

BRAND **AUDIT.**

As we've discussed, no one thinks their kid is ugly. So, when clients come to me asking what they should do about their established brand, it's a tricky conversation. I recognize what has taken them to get their business to the point of coming to me in the first place. I know they birthed their business from a passion, an incident, or a multitude of other reasons. As a result, it's sometimes difficult for them to see their brands objectively. Business owners are passionate creatures, and it's challenging for all of us to shift into a pragmatic mindset to figure out what is in the best interest of each business for growth. Before we make any decisions about how much change is needed for any client's brand, we need a brand audit. A brand audit helps you uncover whether or not:

- Your branding is outdated.
- Your products or services have changed.
- Your current brand is inconsistent.
- You're not reaching your target audience.
- You're preparing for growth.[34]

Once you've gathered all of your information and assessed the strength of your brand you can decide which course of action to take.

RE-FRESH.

Most clients come to me thinking they need to do what I call a re-Fresh. They don't want to change too much if they don't have to, and they want to reduce the risk of there being a disconnect with their loyal customers if they completely re-Brand. But, just because you can still fit into the pair of zebra-print Zubaz you had when you were a senior in high school in 1989 doesn't mean you should.

Unfortunately, often, a re-Fresh doesn't cut the mustard. The reason is because a re-Fresh is very much like changing the color of your lipstick or buying a new tie. You look the same, you live in the same house, but you just needed to . . . well . . . *freshen* things up a bit. If you do a re-Fresh, your business will maintain a visual connection to the look it had before. You might keep your logo but adjust the look, add messaging and update its colors, or expand the components of your design system. Not to mention, some older brands might also need to look at their primary and secondary color palettes to ensure they render across all mediums (particularly when moving from print to web). The color process is very different between the two, as we discussed in chapter 4, so if your colors become an issue, adjusting them can be a relatively easy re-Fresh.

A brand re-Fresh makes perfect sense if your business is humming along, but you feel you need to adjust to compete against your competition, which is moving, as well. By making slight revisions, you can preserve your brand's existing integrity, give it new life, maintain your existing image, and ultimately extend your customer reach.

Do you remember my client and friend, Deb, who owns SAVOR Culinary Services, whom we talked about in chapter 3? She came to me with a very successful business, but she was growing at leaps and bounds. With every new stage of growth, she was putting new messaging into play, but instead of separating them out, her logo began growing "layers"—to the point where it was difficult to decide where to focus. Was her focus culinary services, a mentorship program, or food with purpose?

When she came to me, we decided not to tinker too much with what was working well: her brand recognition. In light of that, we stripped out the "extra" noise from her logo and focused on the core business of "culinary services." The rest of what she does shows up throughout her website, collateral material, and conversations—where it doesn't get in the way of her brand connecting with potential new clients.

Part of the brand re-Fresh my friend Paula (from Hotelements in chapter 2) and I needed to do was to review whereher brand was at the time and where she wanted it to go. She had primarily been focused on the end user (the consumer), but felt she could really make a difference if she could help hoteliers, as well. In doing so, she needed to speak to both groups with one voice— a task which is not always easy when groups' intentions are different. (The hotelier wants to create an experience in their hotels to increase guest attendance. The end user wants to bring that experience home and live it every day.) We deduced a re-Fresh was as far as we needed to take Paula's brand identity. We re-Freshed her mark and converted it to black and white versus full color to neutralize its visual impression while having it feel like the premier brand in the space. It was a clean, fresh home run.

RE-BRAND.

A re-Brand is a little bit of a different story. In this case, a lot changes. Certainly, the visual identity, including the logo, changes, but sometimes the business even gets a new name. As I'm sure you can imagine, this decision does not come lightly. It takes extensive research to determine any large-scale changes are the right course of action, as well as making sure to have a plan in place to ensure the brand pivot will be well received by clients, prospects, and colleagues. Re-Branding is a big deal, so before undertaking one, I make sure my clients view it as such before they move down that path.

Re-Branding begins with analysis of the current marketplace, along with a re-valuation of the competition, businesses operations, target market, and brand message. After surveying your environment, it's imperative to develop a strategy to reach your core audience. Once your plan is laid out, carry out that plan and measure its impact. This last step (measuring the impact) is crucial. Without evaluating what's working and what isn't—and adjusting your methods—all of your re-Branding efforts will fall short.

To get a better idea of what goes into a re-Brand, let's look at Taylor Swift:

> Taylor Swift came onto the music scene as a country girl but, in recent years, has evolved, quite seamlessly, into pop. How did she do it? I spoke with the management firm of some of the most recognized country music entertainers in the business and they shared that Taylor hired a branding firm to make the transition go smoothly to ensure she maintained her original fan base as she grew a new one. To her, pop just felt more "natural," so she took steps to move in that direction. For a while, she had one foot in country and one foot in pop and, to quote her, "If you want to continue to evolve, I think eventually you have to pick a lane, and I just picked the one that felt more natural to me at this point in my life."[35]

A wonderful client of mine is a wealth management firm whom I got to know well during our time working together. I adore the people who work there, and it was the most fun I've had doing my job for as long as I've been doing it. When we began our project, the question of doing a re-Fresh versus a re-Brand was on the table and, after our research, we came to the realization this established firm needed to re-Brand primarily because they needed to speak cross-generationally, with their message resonating from the family patriarch to the Millennial grandchild. As a result, their look, tone, and feel needed to change as well as their messaging. They were open to my recommendations, faith in my ideas and, as a result, this undertaking (as big a project as it was) the client was thrilled with the results.

MICHELLE g

My good friend and client, Michelle, is a marvelous relationship coach. She's one of those people who are so insightful, they've got your number the minute you say, "Hello." It's uncanny how accurate she is when working with her clients. She started out focusing on helping couples with their relationships by getting them in the kitchen and cooking together, but that soon evolved into helping individuals find love because she saw a greater need for singles interested in a relationship and she no longer wanted the entire business model to exclusively revolve around food. As a result of the expansion of her target audience, her brand needed to be reviewed since it had been originally designed to appeal to couples and now had to appeal to both couples and singles. We took a deep dive into what she wanted to accomplish including revising her mission and vision, customer personas, and brand identity. The new logo, including a new color palette, is much stronger—and more generic in focus to allow for the expansion of her brand to include both individuals and couples—food or no food. And the entire brand took on a new identity including a modified point of view to speak to a broader audience.

Re-Branding requires much more than swapping out some color palettes and a re-design of a logo. It's a complete 360-degree turn from the previously established brand. The revisions of the brand stem from a whole new identity through the eyes of all stakeholders. By-products of a re-Brand typically include a new name, terminology, messaging, logo, color scheme(s), and visuals—or some combination thereof. It requires re-evaluating the target audience and speaking directly to them and their needs. Re-Branding makes sense when the business grows and includes additional customer personas or additional products or services from the brand's previous offerings.

When you come out the other side, remember a lot of time and resources have been allotted to this process. So if you go to the trouble of re-Branding, make certain that the changes are genuine—and that you truly live by them.

RE-POSITIONING.

Positioning is one of my favorite parts of my job. I love it because it comes with a powerful ability to influence the masses. When you re-Position a brand, it involves changing what customers associate with that brand—and competing brands. You might change the brand's promise, personality, or tagline (to communicate a new promise), although, often the name and other identity elements don't change drastically.

Let me give you an example from my earliest days at Rollerblade (yes, that Rollerblade). I joined the company when there were fifty-two employees. At the time, they were re-Positioning. The company  had been started to market its product as an off-season cross-training skate for hockey players. The marketing leadership team had decided they wanted to expand their reach further than hockey players, so they re-Positioned themselves as a "lifestyle sport" with a marketing emphasis aimed toward women. How did they do it? By creating a dance performance team, introducing brightly colored skates and apparel, and developing non-hockey related skating events. I was fortunate enough to be part of the event team, and we conducted inline skate races all over the country—even holding one on the track where the Indianapolis 500 takes place. We put Barbie on skates, there was a "Rollerblade baby," and our skates were featured in several movies as well as the 1992 Super Bowl Halftime Show. I believe re-Positioning helped Rollerblade become a household name, and put the company on the map as the pioneers to build the inline skate industry to $1 billion.

Remember my friend, Leo, CEO of Formulaica from chapter 4? He has had some pretty exciting things happening since retiring as an F/A-18 fighter pilot. The creation of his business, where he focuses on digital marketing, was doing well; however, corporate consumers wanted his stories. They wanted his leadership and, even though one of his areas of expertise lies in complex digital marketing campaigns, his ability to focus under astonishing circumstances was creating quite the buzz. He came to me to figure out how he should evolve the company to accommodate the people who were requesting he fill a leadership role. My recommendation was that he re-Position Formulaica to be a personal brand, where he would lead with his leadership skills and offer digital marketing as an ancillary service. He took my advice, and he is now positioned as an influencer in "product creation" and "product launch" in the digital world. His brand has morphed and he is now leading with his personal brand, which is a much stronger play. In this re-Positioning, Leo's business structure changed and logo changed, but his overall palette remained similar.

What should you look for to decide if you should consider a brand re-Positioning? Look for a possible decline in sales, or whether the competition has shifted and morphed in such a way that they have positioned themselves to take market share from you. Doing your work (from chapter 2) will come in handy, here. That data will allow you to determine if re-Positioning is the right play. When it comes to the bottom line, you need to determine what your brand stands for—today. If your brand does not align with your goals and objectives, if you've missed the consumer somehow—if they don't get you or they're not buying—or if you are receiving conflicting feedback, then you need to think about what you want your brand to be, and whether you are delivering the intended benefits.

SO **WHAT?**

Above all, you've got to keep your eyes peeled. Don't rest on your laurels. Each time you think you are done with your brand identity, remind yourself that you're not. Your business is an ever-changing, morphing, evolving brand that needs to speak the language of an audience who is multilingual. Your plans will change, your website will change, your brand identity will be modified, you'll get new headshots, and you'll need to be on your toes so you can circumnavigate the competition and stay in line with your customers.

I was once told by my boss, when I was in the home-building industry, something I will never forget. It was something so simple, yet so profound. I had been recognized as the number-one new home sales person in the nation for several years running. I had won awards and broken records, yet I always had colleagues frustrated with me and trying to fabricate situations of conflict where conflict didn't exist. One day, while we were in his office, he said to me, "Kelly, when you wear the crown, there's always going to be someone trying to knock it off your head." In that moment, I realized you always have to be one step ahead of the competition, of your enemies, and of the marketplace.

BRAND BITS.

- You need to have both a business plan and a marketing plan.
- Your marketing plan needs to be fluid.
- Eye contact and a handshake still mean something.
- Build a "relationship," first, before trying to sell something.
- Event marketing is an important tool in your marketing toolbox.
- People want an experience.
- Go into any event you encounter with goals—and a clear understanding of your opportunity costs.
- Conduct a brand audit regularly.
- When reviewing your brand, consider whether you might benefit from a re-Fresh, re-Brand, or re-Position.
- Your business is ever changing. Keep your eyes on it.

CHAPTER **SEVEN**

MILKING FOR MOO-LAH.

When Joey was a toddler, I was still in my corporate career. He was home with his babysitter when I received a call from her explaining Joey had been crying for the past two hours and she could not figure out why. She said he was pulling his knees up as though he had a tummy ache and she was becoming concerned.

I raced home. When I took him in my arms, he was visibly distressed. I called his pediatrician, but had to leave a message for the doctor to call back. I immediately went into overdrive, trying to figure out how I could provide my son with some relief. I knew he had a history of tummy issues and had been on medications since a very early age to help with reflux, so this felt familiar, but something was off–and I couldn't figure it out. He seemed "fine," but he clearly wasn't. The minutes were ticking by and still I had no call back from his doctor.

I remembered when he was a baby distracting him was very helpful, so I filled a tub full of warm water and decided to put him in the bathtub while we waited for our call. As the tub filled, I sat on the edge and pulled off his shoes. The minute I did, he let out a scream unlike any I've ever heard. I pulled his socks off and his feet were a strange, pale color. Then it dawned on me: his shoes were too small and they were cutting off his circulation.

In that moment, I was devastated. I thought to myself, "How did I miss this? How did I not know my son's shoes no longer fit?" I felt like the worst mother in the world. This little boy who couldn't speak to tell me his shoes were too small was relying on me to take care of him and keep him safe from harm. I had allowed him to cry out in pain because I simply didn't know that his shoes were too small. It bothers me to this day knowing my son was in so much pain and it could have easily been avoided if I had just known.

Why did I share that story? Because, when you start a business, you don't know what you don't know, so how can you ask the right questions if you don't know what you're suppose to ask? I had no reason to think that Joey's feet were cramped in his shoes, so I simply never asked that question. It was a question I had never even thought to ask.

I had a client fly to Minneapolis recently to do a thorough audit on her brand and business that extended over a five-day period. By the end of the second ten-hour day, her face lit up and she said, "I get it! I finally get it." I asked, "What do you get?" And she excitedly replied, "Brand is everything." After two intense days with me, she had her lightbulb moment. She proceeded to say she felt bad she hadn't had that big revelation seven years earlier when she started her business. She confessed: "Had I known this back then, I can't imagine where my business would be today."

When my clients say, "I wish I would have known . . ." or "I had no idea . . ." I try to encourage them by telling them they did the best they could with the information they had at the time. They also wonder why there is no one-stop resource with the formula for the secret sauce of running a business. I have to agree with them that something like that would be helpful.

Even though my son will be twenty years old this year, I'm still frustrated he didn't come into this world with an owner's manual. Raising my son has been much like raising my businesses: lots of twists and turns—and a lot of unknowns. There was a lot of trial and error—and the error part wasn't much fun.

What a relief it is when you get those occasional a-ha moments and you think "Finally!" One of my favorite things Joey says is connected to when we have to do something unpleasant, or when a task winds up being a waste of time. In those situations, he'll say, "Well, that's two hours we can't get back." Every time he says that, it strikes me because of how closely it applies to business practices. We all try so hard to get everything right in business and when something goes wrong we throw up our arms in frustration, do the occasional eye roll, make a few hand gestures, maybe shed some tears, or (if you are like me and my crew) grab a Dammit Doll and give it a few good whacks.

Not knowing what you need to do can be frustrating, which is why I wrote this book. I may not be good at math and I can't save lives, but there are a couple of things I know well, and how to make moo-lah through good branding is one of them. You see, without a brand, a company is worth significantly less. When a brand fails often the business also fails.

Remember my earlier statistic that eight out of ten businesses fail in a given period of time? For those who start a business out of a passion, the business is their hopes and dreams. Its' success or failure affects their families and their livelihoods. I recognized early in life that brand might be the biggest linchpin to a business's success. And, throughout the years, that idea has proven true.

I once heard Matthew Knowles (Beyoncé's dad) speak. He was asked what it was that made some musical acts make it in the entertainment industry and all the others fail, when so many come with such extraordinary talent. He said it could be tied to one common thread: brand. In that single-word answer, he validated what I've been trying to articulate to my clients for years: it's not good enough to have a really great product or service, and it's not good enough we are caring people who want to change the world. We need a solid brand—and brand strategy—to communicate all of our "goodness" and consumer solutions to our audiences so they "feel" the value and benefit we are bringing to their lives.

What happens if you don't know the questions to ask? You need to get in front of people who do know. How do you find these folks? You ask people—a lot of people. Then, once you talk to people, screen their recommendations. I've worked with a lot of people who have spent money on coaches and mentors only to find themselves twelve months down the road in just about the same place they were to begin with—which is not a happy place to be.

At this stage in my career, I am all about trying to share my knowledge and my experiences with other entrepreneurs so maybe they can avoid some of the pitfalls inherent in being in business for yourself. After all, running a business is not for the faint of heart. I once received an amazing piece of advice. It went something like this: "Surround yourself with people smarter than you." With this in mind, I have hired business mentors who have preceded me in that which I aspire to achieve. They have brought with them a level of know-how and encouragement I needed to carve my own path.

As you are putting together your own mentor dream team, consider having a brand strategist as one of the people on your mentor team. He or she will bring you a level of expertise that will complement a business coach as well as your financial support group. Not many people have this person in their camp, so if you bring one on board you'll be ahead of the pack.

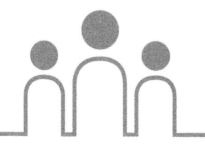

One of my primary goals for **MOO-LAH-GY** was to give you a solid understanding of brand, and the power it has to give you a boost if you build strategically and from a place of understanding. I know chapter 2 was a bugger, but for those who trudged through it, you now have a foundation of information that will help formulate decisions that will be in alignment with your goals and objectives. There is moo-lah on the other side of understanding. If you get your customer and they get you—if you get inside their heads and understand how to solve their problems (and you actually provide the solution)— there will be trust. And remember, on the other side of trust is a sale—which could lead to a raving fan that could lead to residual income and social proof (their talking about you and your product or service through their social circles). And how do we get this trust? By building a relationship that is genuine and authentic in every possible way with each and every client.

Congratulations! You now have an advantage over your competition simply by having read this book. By now, I think it's safe to assume you finally get "it"—or at least part of "it." (And some is better than none.) Remember, part of the point of this book is to demystify branding. If you've had the a-ha moment about what that means, you're already ahead of the majority of folks out there trying to figure it out on their own by throwing a bunch of spaghetti at the wall and hoping some will stick. By reading this book, you've chosen sticky pieces and now you get to throw those. Knowing how to define your brand and create a brand architecture that resonates with—and attracts—your ideal customer is like finding a magic spell. It makes "selling" a whole lot easier when your customers actually understand what they're buying.

But in order to get to that point, you have to do the heady stuff nobody likes to do. It's through the research and the analysis that the impact of brand becomes clear, and clarity helps connect the dots for your customers. Plus, while doing that research, you might actually figure out what makes the most sense—such as choosing a corporate brand or a personal brand—so you can build your brand in a way that gets you noticed.

On the most basic level, just imagine what you can do visually now that you have a solid understanding of how design can support and impact your messaging—and the importance of working with a professional graphic designer. Because so many of us are visual learners, it's imperative your design works succinctly with your business. That cohesion not only gives you a leg up on your competition, it's an absolute and total "dot connector" and when dots connect, sales are made.

Recognizing the difference between brand and marketing will also set you apart. Understanding the visceral impact of your brand on a person's psyche, and how that can be coupled with a tactile marketing plan, simply catapults you to the front of the line. Brands have a measurable monetary value. Remember the Kellogg's study regarding the gold hoop earrings in chapter 1? Brand value can be a positive or a negative, which is why getting it right is so very important.

SO **WHAT?**

So what's the big "So What?" of this book? It might seem obvious, but it's not that simple. The primary takeaway is that you need to have brand trust and a commitment to doing the work. Both are the secret ingredients. Your brand needs to be trustworthy—and that isn't always a static situation. It takes exposure in the right places at the right time, commitment, and the ability to adapt based upon what's important to your audience. The work is just that: work—and it's constant. If you want your brand to be successful, there will be a never-ending laundry list of tasks to do so you can keep the engine oiled and moving down the tracks.

But, you don't have to do it alone. There are additional resources available to you to keep you pushing forward. In fact, if you are still reading this and saying to yourself, "I'm ready to learn more," you can go to my website (kellylucente.com), where you will find a plethora of programs available to you. Some are self-directed activities, and others involve group and/or individual coaching and workshops. I've even created companion workbooks with activities to help you follow through on various sections of this book. You will find them on the "GOODS" page of my website, as follows:

- **BRAND BASICS** continues the conversations from chapter 1 and chapter 5.

- **JUST BUSINESS** covers much of what I talk about (and even more) in heady chapter 2.

- **PERSONAL VS. CORPORATE BRAND** addresses content from chapter 3 in greater detail.

- **ALL THINGS DESIGN** is an extension of chapter 4.

- **EVENTS AND TRADESHOWS** is a deep dive on what we cover in chapter 6.

Regardless of how you proceed down the path of your business venture, be sure to forge ahead with the knowledge that brand—your brand—is important enough to make reading this book worthwhile.

You've got this!
From one business owner to the next, I'm rooting for you! Here's to your continued success.

SNEAK **PEEK**

---

brand·os·o·phy
the science of brand

My next book, **BRANDOSOPHY**, takes a deeper look into the psyche of the consumer and the persuasion of branding as it pertains to attracting an audience to a specific brand–preferably yours. Within that new book, I will explore the difference between a tagline and a slogan, and the power of both. I will talk about how modern trends (or the trends of the day) impact brands.

It's a book that marries proven theory with practical application, through real-time examples of how brand can influence the masses. Using case studies and client and consumer interviews, this book will uncover how you can build a one-of-a-kind, "gotta-have-it" brand.

Here's a brand snack from my next book, **BRANDOSOPHY:**

SNEAK **PEEK**

BRAND CRUSH

I love brands. Everyone who knows me knows it. And one of the things I like to talk about when engaging people in conversation is asking who their brand crush is. When they look at me with the "tilted dog head" look, wondering what I'm asking, I typically say: "A brand crush is a brand that really gets you frothed up. You may not necessarily purchase anything from them, but there is something about the brand that is mesmerizing to you in this moment. I'd love to know which brand does that for you—and why. What is it about that particular brand that makes you stop and say, 'Wow. That's awesome'?"

I go on to explain that this crush could be a company or a person. It could be influenced by their business savvy or their ad campaigns. It could be whatever they want it to be that makes it stand out in their minds. This opens up a very interesting, very fun conversation around what gets people excited behind today's brands. And this conversation helps me get inside the psyche of consumers. Sure, it's a great ice breaker, but learning about the interests of others helps me tweak my brand and offerings to fit what's motivating my audience—now. And, for me, posing questions to get a sense for how they feel about things is another way to research while having fun.

To give you an idea of how this all plays out, I asked some of my friends and clients who their brand crushes were. Here's a couple of their answers:

AMY | previous corporate employee,
now an entrepreneur and CEO of a thriving business

1) Who or what is your brand crush?

My favorite all-time brand is Apple, but my current brand crush would be Taylor Swift. As a business owner and someone who pays attention to personal branding, I am completely in awe of her branding and business savvy.

2) What do you like about it specifically that makes it your current crush?

Honestly, there are too many things to list, but here are a few:

- She controls her personal brand like a master.
- She is one of the most powerful woman in music, but you don't hear about her out partying, being a diva, or doing things that would make her look like someone you wouldn't like.
- She controls how her image is used and has gone as far as copyrighting a number of small snippets of her lyrics to be able to control how they are used in merchandising.
- Her target market tends to be teenage girls and pre-teen girls. She is always dressed modestly and portrays herself in a way that most mothers would be happy for their teen girls to emulate.
- Her concerts are always sold out and, when she came to San Diego, most of the moms were just as excited to go see her show as their daughters were.

3) What is it about this brand that speaks to you?

I love how she used her influence to fight for musicians and not allow companies like Spotify to devalue what the artists are doing. I feel like, in a day of all-access, all-the-time via the Internet, it is important for the creators of value to be rewarded for the value they create!

But most of all, it is how she uses social media and grassroots marketing to interact with her fans and make them feel important. When she released her most recent album, she hosted listening parties for her fans in her homes around the country. Can you imagine what it would have felt like for these young girls to be invited to her home? She is constantly making her fans' dreams come true by inviting them to concerts, visiting sick fans, and more.

I read an article this morning that she brought one of her fans to her concert in Australia. But the thing that spoke volumes is that this little girl was losing her hearing and she wanted to experience a Taylor Swift concert while she could still hear. I love how she is constantly trying to touch her fans.

Also, this seems to be one of the most hardworking young women around. Each time she releases an album, she is EVERYWHERE promoting it! She doesn't just expect it to sell, she works for it.

4) How does this brand make you "feel"? How does it move you?

I am not the typical Taylor Swift target demographic. I have never bought one of her full albums or paid for a concert ticket, but I am always just in awe and admiration of Taylor and her business savvy. I don't know if it is her or if it is her team, but they understand how to be known for doing good. There are often times that I read a story about this young woman that make me cry. For an artist of her success and stature, she has made herself very accessible to her fans, which I admire greatly!!!

5) If you were on their branding team, what one thing would you suggest they do to enhance what they already have built?

I would love to see her do more collaborations. She is a talented songwriter and an amazing businesswoman. I feel that, by doing more collaboration, she could potentially expand her audience base. But, ultimately, what she's doing seems to be working pretty darn well for her. So maybe, if it isn't broke, don't fix it.

CHRISTINE | Entrepreneur and
CEO Ghost Writer to the stars

1) Who or what is your brand crush?

Disney.

2) What do you like about it specifically that makes it your current crush?

More so than any other brand, it elicits an incredibly powerful brand feeling and almost visceral experience to the core of my being. I see anything Disney, hear the word, or see those mouse ears, and I am instantly transported to a happy, joyful place of dreaming, imagination, fun, and endless possibility. They have nailed "brand feeling" as far as I am concerned. And it's more than a current crush, it is a 40+-year crush.

3) What is it about this brand that speaks to you?

Everything I just said.

4) How does this brand make you "feel"? How does it move you?

Disney moves me into action in my own life. When I hear "if you can dream it then you can do it," it's not just a line pertaining to Disney for me, it's a mantra that I have adopted into my own life. It gives me permission to dream big and imagine without boundaries.

5) If you were on their branding team, what one thing would you suggest they do to enhance what they already have built?

Other than keeping theme park tickets within the realm of the upper middle class, I would just hope that they never lose that dreaming, imagining spirit that Walt Disney built the brand on, all those decades ago. With a brand built so powerfully on an emotion, I understand this is a risk. Brand—at the level of infusion throughout every strand of employee culture, training, product development, and every inch of the corporation—is crucial to making sure they don't stray too far from their roots. Because [if it changed] their brand fans would sense it in an instant. The emotion would shift—and that could easily be the beginning of the end for them.

So, what can we learn from these two brand crush examples? They both vary greatly from one another not to mention there is a variety of opinion around what sparked their reasons for choosing their brand crush. If we were to choose one of the brand crushes listed above and ask the other person about the other's crush, the comments would be all over the board. Each person has their own unique spin on what gets them excited about a particular brand. Our goal as business owners is to be able to define our differences and similarities so we can develop our own brand, one that appeals to our specified demographic. For example, Amy's brand crush, Taylor Swift is a caring, philanthropic person and artist and she has a specific point of view and stands behind it in everything she does. Amy likes Taylor's bold and steadfast approach to having a point of view and her caring nature because Amy defines herself similarly and exudes a similar drive. Christine is in awe of her crush because Disney represents everything she stands for in her life and business. She can see her own life through the eyes of her brand crush and sits in total appreciate of Walt Disney's innovation and vision. Both women have very clear reasons for their choices, but keep in mind their opinions might change down the road. There might be another brand that catches their fancy. Even though their crushes might change, keep in mind the underlying philosophy in what appeals to them will remain the same. If you ask either woman to list their top five crushes, you'd most definitely see an underlying pattern. Notice Amy said her "all time favorite" crush was Apple. What are some similarities between Taylor Swift and Apple besides the open letter Taylor wrote to Apple criticizing their new streaming music?[35] Well, they both want to do the right thing as the resolution regarding the streaming music issue demonstrated. Both want to continue to push what's expected and safe. And, both are innovators. Do you see the pattern?

The brand crush exercise can be fun and extremely informative. You can use it as a means to collect preference data to tailor marketing and branding efforts to your audience and really explore the psychology of branding which is what **BRANDOSOPHY** is all about. I encourage you to give it a try for yourself. You never know what you might conclude from the experience.

If you liked this excerpt of **BRANDOSOPHY** and want to learn more, go to (**kellylucente.com**).

END**NOTES**

(1) History of Crayola, last modified 2013, http://www.cray-ola.com/about-us/company/history.aspx

(2) Walsh, Tim, *Timeless Toys: Classic Toys and the Playmakers Who Created Them*, (Andrews McMeel Publishing, 2005), 71

(3) "42 Impressive Logos & Identity Design Projects", Jessica Farris, July 24, 2015, http://www.howdesign.com/design-creativity/award-winning-brand-identity-design/

(4) "A Brief History of Branding", Matt Shadel, January 8, 2014, https://www.weareconvoy.com/2014/01/a-brief-history-of-branding/

(5) Calkins, Tim and Alice Tybout (editors), *Kellogg on Branding: The Marketing Faculty of The Kellogg School of Management* (Wiley, 2005), 3

(6) "Leaning Tower of Pisa-Brief Construction History", last modified 2015, http://madridengineering.com/case-study-the-leaning-tower-of-pisa/

(7) Wikinvest, last modified January 4, 2016, http://www.wikinvest.com/stock/General_Mills_(GIS)

(8) "The most-liked advertising slogan: M&M's 'Melts in your mouth, not in your hand'", Justin Wm. Moyer, June 24, 2014, https://www.washingtonpost.com/news/morning-mix/wp/2014/06/24/the-most-liked-advertising-slogan-mms-melts-in-your-mouth-not-in-your-hand/

(9) "The Wartime Origins of the M&M", Laura Schumm, June 2, 2014, http://www.history.com/news/hungry-history/the-wartime-origins-of-the-mm

(10) Franklin D. Roosevelt Presidential Library and Museum Website, http://www.fdrlibrary.marist.edu/aboutfdr/polio.html

(11) "7 Things You Can Do To Build An Awesome Personal Brand", Shama Hyder, August 18, 2014, http://www.forbes.com/sites/shamahyder/2014/08/18/7-things-you-can-do-to-build-an-awesome-personal-brand/

(12) "What's the difference between Personal branding & Professional branding?", Sara Rosso, July 17, 2013, http://whenihavetime.com/2013/07/17/whats-the-difference-between-personal-branding-professional-branding/

(13) Godin, Seth, *Tribes: We Need You to Lead Us*, (Portfolio, 2008)

(14) "Numbers You Should Know Regarding Sales", Referral Squirrel, 2013, http://thereferralsquirrel.com/numbers-you-should-know/

(15) "Why Is Facebook Blue? The Science Behind Colors In Marketing", Leo Widrich, May 6, 2013, http://www.fastcompany.com/3009317/why-is-facebook-blue-the-science-behind-colors-in-marketing

(16) "The Top Three Reasons Why New Products Fail", Victor Covone, July 28, 2015, http://www.rdmag.com/articles/2015/07/top-three-reasons-why-new-products-fail

(17) "Remembering Gary Dahl, the Marketing Magician Who Made Millions Selling Pet Rocks", Geoff Weiss, April 1, 2015, http://www.entrepreneur.com/article/244602

(18) Wheeler, Alina, *Designing Brand Identity: An Essential Guide for the Whole Branding Team*, (John Wiley and Sons, 2012), 16

(19) "The World's Most Valuable Brands", 2015 Ranking, http://www.forbes.com/powerful-brands/list/

(20) "Life Is Good: Powered By People, Fueled By Optimism", David Aponovich, July 18, 2012, http://www.fastcompany.com/1842834/life-good-powered-people-fueled-optimism

(21) "Better Than Fast Food", Katy Waldman, October 12, 2012, http://www.slate.com/articles/business/the_pivot/2012/10/where_s_the_beef_how_wendy_s_1980s_turnaround_changed_the_fast_food_business_.html

(22) LinkedIn Higher Education Website, last modified 2015, https://university.linkedin.com/content/dam/university/global/en_US/site/pdf/TipSheet_BuildingYourBrand.pdf

(23) "Branding vs. Marketing", Matchstic.com, http://match-stic.com/thinking/branding-vs-marketing

(24) "Starbucks Launches First Brand Campaign, 'Meet Me at Starbucks'", Maureen Morrison, September 29, 2014, http://adage.com/article/cmo-strategy/starbucks-launches-brand-campaign/295175/

(25) "Branding vs. Advertising: Know the Difference to Grow", Chris Garrett, February 28, 2014, http://brandtwist.com/advertising/branding-vs-advertising-know-the-differ-ence-to-grow/

(26) "How generating more Love for your brand will make You More Money", Graham Robertson, November 19, 2013, http://beloved-brands.com/2013/11/19/brand-love/

(27) "The QSR 50: The 50 brands setting the pace in the quick-service and fast-casual restaurant industries", Sam Oches, August 2013, https://www.qsrmagazine.com/re-ports/qsr50-2013-top-50-chart

(28) "Marketing Plan Template: Exactly What To Include", Dave Lavinsky, September 30, 2013, http://www.forbes.com/sites/davelavinsky/2013/09/30/marketing-plan-template-exactly-what-to-include/2/

(29) "Premature Solicitation – Don't Get Caught Out", Dr Ivan Misner, August 2015, http://www.brandquar-terly.com/premature-solicitation-dont-get-caught?utm_source=ReviveOldPost&utm_medium=social&utm_campaign=ReviveOldPost

(30) "The IMAX Difference", accessed December 2015, http://www.imax.com/content/imax-difference

(31) "Explore the Strategy of Event Marketing", Marketing-Schools.org, http://www.marketing-schools.org/types-of-marketing/event-marketing.html

(32) "Minnesota State Fair Detailed Daily Attendance", http://www.mnstatefair.org/general_info/attendance.html

(33) "When to Hold Your Seminar: Which Day of the Week Is Best for Your Seminar?", Jenny Hamby, http://www.self-growth.com/articles/when-to-hold-your-seminar-which-day-of-the-week-is-best-for-your-seminar

(34) "Is it time for a brand refresh?", Bethany Howell, http://www.insight180.com/is-it-time-for-a-brand-refresh/

(35) "Taylor Swift and Apple: The back story", Michal Lev-Ram, July 14, 2015, http://fortune.com/2015/07/14/taylor-swift-apple-backstory/

ABOUT THE **AUTHOR**

Kelly Lucente is CEO of Re-Tool Marketing, a creative agency that focuses on growing brands, building strategies, and identifying positioning for entrepreneurs and small to mid-sized corporations. She also heads up Bubble Print Press, a book publishing company that offers full-service brand and marketing assistance for those who want to tell their story to the world.

A 25 + year veteran in both marketing and sales, Kelly has worked with Fortune 500 brands, most notably the Ryland Group, Pulte Group, RE/MAX, and Pearle Vision. She was one of the marketing team members of Rollerblade – a company that helped build the inline skate industry to $1 Billion and turned Rollerblade into a household name. She has also worked with Mattamy Homes, Canada's largest homebuilder. She created the children's educational product, Bye Bye Monster that was featured in Neiman Marcus and has partnered with celebrities such as Jenny McCarthy as a contributor to her Generation Rescue Foundation.

Kelly has won both Gold and Silver National Association of Home Builders Salesperson of the Year Awards four times in consecutive years and Dr. Toy Awards twice for product innovation.

Kelly plays an integral role at her agency as lead brand strategist and creative director. She focuses on shaping client engagement and spearheads all strategic innovation to transform corporate brands. Her expertise is helping businesses attract the right customer, gain market share, and increase revenue.

She wrote **MOO-LAH-GY** to share the secret sauce of branding that many of her clients fly to Minnesota in minus 45 degrees wind-chill to get.

Kelly divides her time between Re-Tool Marketing and her personal brand, Kelly Lucente, which focuses on client initiative, small-group workshops, books on brand, and keynote speaking. Outside of work, Kelly enjoys time with her family (especial-

ly her son, Joey) and giving back to her community as an active member of Children's Hospital and Clinics of Minnesota Foundation, as an advisory board member for the Entrepreneurship Class at the University of Minnesota Carlson School of Management, and as a mentor for the MN Cup, a statewide, new-venture competition for entrepreneurs.

You can reach Kelly through Re-Tool Marketing at (**retoolmarketing.com**) or via her personal brand website, Kelly Lucente at (**kellylucente.com**).

Kelly Lucente

CPSIA information can be obtained
at www.ICGtesting.com
Printed in the USA
BVOW08s0450150218
508100BV00002B/404/P